# Philosophy
## A Beginner's Guide

**ONEWORLD BEGINNER'S GUIDES** combine an original, inventive, and engaging approach with expert analysis on subjects ranging from art and history to religion and politics, and everything in between. Innovative and affordable, books in the series are perfect for anyone curious about the way the world works and the big ideas of our time.

# Philosophy
## A Beginner's Guide

Peter Cave

ONEWORLD

A Oneworld Paperback Original

Published by Oneworld Publications 2012

Reprinted 2013

Copyright © Peter Cave 2011

The moral right of Peter Cave to be identified as the Author
of this work has been asserted by him in accordance with
the Copyright, Designs and Patents Act 1988

All rights reserved
Copyright under Berne Convention
A CIP record for this title is available
from the British Library

ISBN 978-1-85168-937-8
ISBN 978-1-78074-116-1 (ebook)

Typeset by Cenveo Publisher Services, Bangalore, India
Cover design by vaguelymemorable.com
Printed and bound in Denmark by Nørhaven A/S

Oneworld Publications
10 Bloomsbury Street
London WC1B 3SR
UK

Stay up to date with the latest books,
special offers, and exclusive content from
Oneworld with our monthly newsletter

Sign up on our website
**www.oneworld-publications.com**

Dedicated to those who do not know
– including –
those who do not know they do not know

# Contents

# Contents

# PHILOSOPHERS ON PHILOSOPHY

The unexamined life is not worth living.

Socrates (469–399BC)

Other people may well be unaware that all who actually engage in philosophy aright are practising nothing other than dying and being dead.

Plato (429–347BC)

Curiosity first led men to philosophize and that still leads them.

Aristotle (384–322BC)

Philosophy is properly home-sickness; the wish to be everywhere at home.

Novalis (1772–1801)

To repeat the whole nature of the world abstractly, universally, and distinctly in concepts, and thus to store up, as it were, a reflected image of it in permanent concepts always at the command of reason; this and nothing else is philosophy.

Schopenhauer (1788–1860)

A philosophical problem has the form: I don't know my way about.
   The problems are solved, not by giving new information, but by arranging what we have always known.
   Philosophy is a battle against the bewitchment of our intelligence by means of language.

Wittgenstein (1889–1951)

A philosopher is like a blind man in a dark room looking for a black cat... that is not there.

Anon

# Prologue:
## take your time

Philosophy is the child of wonder – of wonder and curiosity about the world. The world, of course, consists not solely of what we are able to perceive – see, hear, smell, touch and taste – but also of our thoughts, desires and imagination: of ourselves. The self and its awareness of the world generate wonder, curiosity and also bafflement. What is the self? What is the reality behind appearances?

We seek to understand the world, including ourselves, through science, mathematics and reason, through art, music and religion. We also act on the world, change the world and feel that some things ought to be done, while others ought not. We possess a sense of morality, of the good and the bad, of how societies need scope for liberty, welfare and justice, of how lives may possess – or lack – meaning.

Philosophers philosophize about all the matters just mentioned. Philosophers philosophize not just about the reality of the physical world and ourselves, but also about how we gain knowledge of the world and the nature of scientific theories about that world. Philosophers also reflect on quite what goes on in other areas of study and activity – in mathematics, physics and psychology; plays, poetry, art and music.

The philosopher is not a citizen of any community of ideas.
That is what makes him into a philosopher.

Those are words from the Cambridge philosopher Ludwig Wittgenstein, arguably the greatest philosopher of the twentieth century. They tell us that philosophers may focus their thinking – and thinking is at the heart of philosophizing – on any arena. Thus, philosophers investigate the nature of mind, of time and action; they consider attempted proofs for God's existence, arguments about free will – and whether goodness and beauty are objective. Thinking philosophically is not quick and easy. Thinking hard can sometimes be as tiring as manual labour, though hands remain clean, and the thinking may well be accompanied by a glass of wine – or two.

The classical image, caricature indeed, of a philosopher is of Socrates wandering ancient Athens, head in clouds. In fact, Socrates was firmly earthbound: his philosophical beginnings were curiosities raised by everyday life – by what people did and said, and by their relationships. Some individuals are praised as courageous, virtuous and knowledgeable: they desire love, beauty and truth. So, Socrates would ask his famous 'What is?' questions. What is courage – virtue, knowledge? What is justice – beauty, truth? He was adept at showing the show-offs that, in the end, they did not know. Hence, there is Socrates' quip that he was considered the wisest man of Athens because he knew that he did not know – well, let us assume he added *sotto voce*, apart from knowing that he did not know.

Now, it is a substantial philosophical question how questions of the Socratic form should be answered. Consider: 'What is beauty?' Socrates and others assumed that items of beauty must possess a certain quality in common, running throughout, making them all beautiful. Wittgenstein – yes, his name will appear quite a few times – famously drew attention to 'family resemblances', suggesting that often a term is correctly applied to a group of items, even though there is no single thread running throughout, justifying use of that term. A rope is strong because of the overlapping of weak threads. Consider all the different activities that are games. Must they have something in common, running through them all, that makes them all games?

Those few thoughts above have already edged us into some philosophizing, into a metaphysical puzzle, one concerning so-called universals. The flag, grass and emeralds are all green; they possess that similarity. Does that show that a 'universal' greenness somehow has being and is manifested in different places and times, in a flag here and grass there? That type of consideration led Plato into his Theory of Forms: Plato turns his eyes from the ever-changing physical world to an inspiring vision of eternal abstractions or forms. Plato focused on, for example, justice, beauty, truth, equality – but, as he later recognized, his approach could also lead, unhappily lead, to eternal forms of dirt, hair and mud – and worse.

Philosophy is associated with wisdom: etymologically, the term 'philosophy' is derived from the Greek, meaning 'lover of wisdom'. 'Wisdom' conveys a feeling of something grander, deeper and more insightful about life and the universe than worldly investigations undertaken by, for example, archaeologists, psychologists and physicists. Of course, we speak of insights gained through poetry, fiction and religion; but Western philosophy typically differs from those approaches – and hence from much of Eastern philosophy and, indeed, postmodernist writings – by paying attention to argument, clarity, the highlighting of assumptions. The results can be different ways of looking at how things must be, different perspectives on how things ought to be.

The purveyance of wisdom may seem far removed from the practice of today's philosophers; they are usually university lecturers, ever concerned to satisfy funding demands and preserve jobs by publishing more and more articles, with increasing citations and bibliographies. It was different in earlier times. Francis Bacon was Lord Chancellor and imprisoned; Spinoza ground lenses; Leibniz was a diplomat, then librarian. John Stuart Mill worked for the East India Company, moonlighting as a journalist, and was later a Member of Parliament. Today there is also increasing specialization in philosophy, as if it is a scientific subject, accessible to few. Examine current volumes of academic philosophy: you will often encounter abstruse arguments, technical terms and sometimes unusual symbols. Now, some good philosophy can be done that way, particularly in logical studies, but it should not mislead us into thinking that, at heart, philosophy is a technical subject, impossible to understand except by professionals.

For centuries, many great philosophical thinkers were as much exercised by mathematics and the sciences as by philosophical perplexities. Philosophers such as Aristotle, Descartes, Spinoza and Leibniz conducted empirical researches; Descartes and Leibniz were also highly important mathematicians. Philosophers, though, when philosophizing, are not scientists – though they will take into account scientific discoveries and concepts. For example, should electrons be thought of as existing just as tables and chairs do – or are they mere theoretical tools, useful in making predictions? Philosophers do not risk physical explosions by working in laboratories, or broken limbs from archaeological diggings.

Philosophers often explore concepts and concerns of which we are all aware – be it in Ancient Greece, twenty-first century Europe or a South American tribe. Whoever we are, wherever we are, we speak of the truth, of knowledge, of thoughts. Whoever we are, wherever we are, we notice conflicts between our desires, talk about fairness and sometimes worry about life being pointless.

Philosophers reason. Philosophy is largely an *a priori* subject, one that relies on our powers of reasoning about our concepts, beliefs and assumptions, not on further empirical worldly research. Contradictions may be exposed, arguments revealed as fallacious and conceptual revisions encouraged. This book, then, is an introduction to Western philosophy, with the emphasis on reason and argument. That does not mean demoting the value of emotions, of beauty, of meaning; they can be reasoned about without devaluation. Furthermore, we should recognize that any philosophical stance may well itself be grounded in emotion. After all, truth-seekers possess the emotional desire for truth.

Although this is an introductory text, instead of laboriously going through numerous terms and theories – after all, there are many fine dictionaries and encyclopaedias (see notes and further reading) – I have deliberately focussed on some major themes, with deep and troubling problems, often with direct relevance to everyday life. Sometimes I have taken a position. As a result, readers will end up encountering important theories and ideas, as well as influential philosophers. The overall approach is to provide a flavour of the problems, a flavour that will stimulate thought and encourage further reading.

A philosophical work should not be read as a novel. Chapters may be skimmed to gain a 'feel' for the problems; but then particular thoughts and questions need to be mulled over, be it in the bath, on the train or as a way of falling asleep or (more likely, I hope) of being kept awake.

'All things conspire' wrote Hippocrates, pointing to how problems interconnect and can reappear in different contexts. This introduction to philosophy celebrates that fact; it has been deliberately framed so that certain concepts and problems that may initially seem obscure reappear in new areas and under fresh perspectives, aiding understanding. Chapter One, in particular, introduces matters that are delved into further in later chapters.

$$\Upsilon$$

The best way into philosophy is to engage in the activity oneself. Although there are many right and wrong answers in philosophy, with the deepest problems it is often a matter of endeavouring to see the world in a certain light, engaging problems in ways that harmonize with other beliefs and ways of seeing.

Philosophers have often said very odd things, but, dig a
little deeper, and we can usually find some good reasons.
The philosophical wonder and curiosity led some Pre-Socratics –
those ancient Greek philosophers prior to Socrates – suggesting
very different realities behind appearances. 'Everything is in flux'
said Heraclitus, yet, on the contrary, argued Parmenides, 'What is,
must be indestructible and deathless'. In more recent centuries,
we meet Spinoza arguing that God and Nature are one and the
same, Berkeley trying to persuade us that physical objects are
nothing but collections of mind-dependent ideas, and, advancing
to early twentieth-century Cambridge, we find McTaggart arguing that time is sheer illusion – though, as G. E. Moore would
quip, no doubt he had his breakfast *before* he had his lunch.

Philosophers are keen to follow the argument where it takes
them. That is one of the many fascinations in thinking things
through – in philosophizing. There are no quick fixes in philosophy. Thinking deeply about matters, weaving musings into a
coherent whole, takes time. And so, how can I resist a last com-
ment in this preface from Wittgenstein? When two philosophers
meet, said the anguished genius, they should greet each other
with the words, 'Take your time.'

In reading about philosophy, in doing philosophy – in
philosophizing – take your time.

# PHILOSOPHERS OF ANCIENT GREECE

**Socrates, Plato, Aristotle** – this Athenian triumvirate – are of astonishing and continuing influence over Western philosophy – metaphysics, epistemology, ethics, political philosophy and, one-time, the sciences when subsumed as 'natural philosophy'.

Socrates (469–399BC) was an intellectual gadfly, stinging the complacency of the rich and powerful – of those who thought they knew. Found guilty of corrupting the young and of impiety, he was sentenced to death by hemlock, and declined to escape. Most of what we know about him derives from his greatest pupil, Plato.

Plato (429–347BC): all subsequent philosophy has been described as a footnote to Plato. Plato looked beyond this world of ever-changing appearances, to unchanging 'forms' or ideas. He suggested recipes for the good life, radical ideas for society – women on a par with men – and offered thoughts on love, desire and mind.

Aristotle (384–322BC), Plato's greatest pupil, was the first formal logician, engaged in considerable scientific researches, and even taught Alexander who became Alexander the Great. In Raphael's painting *The School of Athens*, Plato points upwards and Aristotle downwards – for Plato sought reality beyond appearances, arguably with a touch of mysticism, whereas Aristotle was down to earth.

**The Pre-Socratics** are philosophers prior to Socrates. Much of their work is lost but they were highly influential – two notables being Heraclitus and Parmenides. Heraclitus – the enigmatic – announced that you cannot step into the same river twice for waters are always changing. A quick response is: you cannot even step into the same river once. Parmenides, in a poem, *The Way Truth*, argued that all is one and unchanging. It met support via Zeno of Elea's motion paradoxes: how can you reach that wall? First you need to go halfway, then half of the remainder, then half the new remainder... and so on. Those halves of half, although ever teenier, go on endlessly, infinitely – thus, they cannot be completed.

## Lest we are misled

Philosophers can be easily forgotten, when focus is on the greats. Other important philosophers include Protagoras – 'man is the measure' – later, the Stoics and Epicureans. Away from ancient Greece are St Augustine, the highly influential St Aquinas, and a medley of medieval logicians such as William of Ockham.

# 1

# What is it to be human?

'We should live just for experiences,' say some. That strikes many as shallow for there is more to life than experiences; after all, we ought to be eager that the lives of others go well. 'Yet surely,' comes the response, 'their lives going well is solely a matter of their having experiences as desired.'

Suppose you are being betrayed – so-called friends speak badly of you behind your back; your partner deceives you – yet you are totally unaware of what is really happening and will never find out. Your life strikes you as going well, so well. Your experiences are just as they would be, were you not being betrayed. Even though you will never find out, is your life *really* going well in the way that you would wish? Would you not prefer a life in which you were not deceived?

Such questions lead to philosophical reflections and troubling depths. True, human life would not count for much, to say the least, if it lacked all experience; but arguably it needs more – and being human, we recognize and value the more. Being human, we are capable of reflection on the distinction between appearance and reality, between how things strike us – experiences of friendly, smiling faces; declarations of love and fidelity – and how things really are, such as undiscovered betrayal.

γ

The above musings will lead us into philosophical arguments on the values and nature of human beings – on our 'selves' – via a much discussed 'experience machine' example, and the famous, nay infamous, Monsieur Descartes, the so-called 'father of modern philosophy'. They set the scene for later chapters, where those and related problems are further explored. 'Modern' for philosophers, by the way, curiously commences in the early seventeenth century, when, at least superficially, Descartes focused on understanding the world solely through reason, without reliance on classical, Aristotelian or biblical authority and when, a little earlier, Francis Bacon encouraged scientific experimentation for grasping the world's workings.

## The experience machine – and what matters

Suppose you would love to sail, single-handedly, round the world, but you are lazy, lack the stamina and, for that matter, easily fall prey to seasickness. Suppose too that there is a machine, a virtual reality machine, a dream machine – *an experience machine* – that will provide you with any experiences ordered. Once plugged into the machine, you are unable to tell that you are on the machine, unable to remember that you requested the machine; instead you undergo all the required experiences, feelings, beliefs, indistinguishable from the real thing. Would you be getting what you wanted?

From 'within', from your experiences, all appears just as if actually travelling the oceans. You have the experiences, it seems to you, of the ocean's swell, the distant lands and some seasickness (though mildly presented, according to your pre-plugging requests) – experiences of beautiful maidens or handsome gentlemen welcoming you at ports, of media quayside interviews – yet all the time you are stretched out, let us suppose, in some grubby basement quarter, be it in London, New York or Delhi, plugged into the machine.

To date, such machines are technologically impossible; but there is nothing impossible – no contradiction – in the supposition of electrodes plugged into your brain, feeding you appropriate electro-chemical impulses and thereby the experiences mentioned. Such suppositions are now common fare in certain popular films – *The Matrix* is a typical example – with tales of virtual realities. What is the philosophical value of such thought-experiments? Well, one value is that they aid focus on what is distinctive about, and important in, human life.

Suppose that you could have access to such a machine, one that would deliver all the experiences that you sought, without your even needing to crawl out of bed. Would you be getting what you wanted, if suitably plugged? Are the important and valuable things in life solely matters of experiences?

The answer, for many, is 'no' – an answer encouraged by the betrayal example above. True, we can be eager just for certain experiences – we may enjoy tingles of pleasure – whatever the source. We sometimes desire certain distinctive contents to experiences – sounds of a flute or scents of freshly mown grass – without regard to whether they are actually caused by a flute or grass, or by some electronic machine. Most of the time, though, we have an interest in 'outreach', in touching what is real, in our experiences being of the real thing. The experience machine fails to deliver on that score: the experiences are real enough, but what they are *of* is not the real world.

Yes, we may long to know how it feels from within to be sailing the world's oceans; yet that is not actually to be sailing the world's oceans. I may make do with imaginary experiences of being a world-class pianist, yet what I truly want is to be a pianist in reality, with audience appreciation and garlands. People typically yearn for love, for children – to watch sports with their teams winning. They are not yearning solely for experiences *as if* of love, children, and wins: they want the real un-faked thing – and here is the rub – even though they cannot tell the difference between the experience *as if* of X and an experience really of X. People typically want to achieve things: on the machine they receive mere illusions of achievement. They do not win the race; it merely appears to them as if they win.

## Existing without the body – as a mind, self or soul?

Tales of betrayal and of experience machines encourage the thought that what is valuable to humans is not solely experiential. The tales, though, may lead us to wonder how we secure a grip, if we do, on anything existing beyond our experiences. Indeed, how do we know that we are not already on experience machines – maybe having made bad pre-plugging selections of experiences, such as reading philosophy? That latter question raises the intense pressure of scepticism, of doubting whether, for example, we can ever have knowledge of reality. That is an epistemic question, 'epistemic' from the Greek for knowledge. The sceptical problem is explored in a later chapter; here, we shall see how Descartes uses scepticism to uncover what human beings essentially are. Let us gently lead into an understanding of his argument.

In undergoing experiences and holding values, clearly we are conscious beings; but what are we, we who suffer the undergoing and holding? We each have a head and a heart (the latter at least literally), but what are we essentially? That is, what *must* we have – logically, necessarily – in order to exist? Reflect: millions of people believe in the possibility of survival after bodily death, even of survival without a body at all; but are those really logical possibilities, possibilities lacking contradiction? It is logically impossible for a triangle, Euclidean, to have four sides; such a triangle cannot exist without having three sides. Is it similarly logically impossible for you to exist without a human body? Might a human be essentially a soul without need of body?

### 'THE FATHER OF MODERN PHILOSOPHY'

**René Descartes** (1596–1650) is deemed the father for he started afresh in trying to establish knowledge, what is certain and cannot be doubted, without appeal to ancient or religious authority. He encouraged reflective readers to take up the project, the order of discovery being shown in his six *Meditations on First Philosophy*.

**Life:** Descartes, as a young man, travelled – he joined an army for that purpose – and in 1619, in a stove-filled room, dreamt of constructing a wonderful new understanding of the world. He laid the foundations for analytical geometry – hence *Cartesian* coordinates – worked on optics and astronomy and sought to explain the physical world and the human body in mathematical mechanical terms. The mind – the soul – he saw as distinct from the body.

He was set to publish a work on the world, suggesting the Earth orbited the Sun, but, on hearing about Galileo's condemnation by the Church, he withdrew. Although a Catholic believer, he was often attacked for his mechanistic philosophy; rumours were apparently sown concerning a mechanical doll he invented.

**Demise:** Descartes' fame spread and Queen Christina of Sweden asked him to tutor her. One cannot decline royal 'invitations' and Descartes, in any case keen on patronage, ended up in a Stockholm winter. Tragically for one who would rise after noon, tutorials were at 5.00 am. Descartes soon died from pneumonia.

The experience machine shows how things may not be as they seem. Suggesting something far more radical than that thought experiment, Descartes argued that we can doubt the existence of *all* material items – of trees and turnips; of land and lakes; of marmalade… and machines. We may be dreaming that such things exist. For that matter, an all-powerful evil genius may be deceiving us. Who knows? That evil genius may also mislead us into believing that we have limbs, organs and brains. After all, there are real cases of 'phantom limbs': people awake after surgery, feeling pleased. 'From within' it feels as if their legs were not amputated – yet when they remove the sheets, they find themselves legless (literally so). They feel pains where their legs should have been; in fact their legs are miles away in an incinerator.

Scepticism about what really is so does not require the possibility of powerful cleverness and malignant motivation. Simply reflect: we assume an external physical world exists which causes our experiences. Perhaps, though, as with the experience machine, the cause of our experiences is something completely different from what we think. Perhaps our experiences are caused by nothing at all; they just happen. Those suggestions appear as logical possibilities, however unlikely in fact. Indeed, how could we even assess that likelihood?

I have spoken of Descartes and used 'we'; but the discussion needs the first person – *I* – for just as I may doubt the existence of an external physical world, so I may doubt the existence of other people. That is the sceptical problem of 'other minds': even if other human bodies exist – something that may be doubted – there is a further level of doubt: namely, what justifies my belief that there are minds 'behind' such bodies? It is surely possible, or so it appears, that those others are nothing but bodies, lacking all consciousness. Maybe you are the sole conscious being in the universe, these words having been generated, printed and transported by mechanical robots or by creatures, 'zombies', without experiences; it is you who gives meaning to the words.

After his sceptical reflections, Descartes concludes that even if the external world, the physical world, does not exist – even if he is radically deceived – still he must exist. However hard an evil genius may deceive him, he, Descartes, would have to exist to be deceived. The underlying thought is that while he can feign – pretend, imagine – that the external world lacks existence, he cannot feign that he lacks existence. From this derives his famous 'I think, therefore I am' – 'cogito ergo sum' – abbreviated to the *cogito*. One argument lurking here – Descartes' Feigning Argument – popped into the first person is the following:

Premiss 1:    My body (including brain) can be feigned by me not to exist.

Premiss 2:    I (whatever I am) cannot be feigned by me not to exist.

Conclusion:    Therefore, my body is not identical with me (the 'I', whatever it is that I am).

Descartes' conclusion leads to the possibility, but only the possibility, of his surviving after his body's destruction. Descartes does, in fact, offer a quick argument for immortality, though with a caveat. An item, he claims, can be destroyed only either by being broken into parts or by annihilation courtesy of God, an omnipotent being. The mind – the I – is indivisible: the mind lacks parts. I can make no sense of my being simultaneously two distinct consciousnesses. Hence, eternal survival is guaranteed – so long as God sustains.

How are we to understand the Feigning Argument? Here is an approach. Suppose you have heard talk of Belle and of Tinkers. You are wondering whether they are one and the same person possessing two names. Well, one way of establishing that they are distinct is by discovering that Belle has a property that Tinkers lacks. If right now Belle is in New York and Tinkers in Calcutta, then they cannot be one and the same. We assume that one and the same single human being cannot be stretched miles across continents and oceans.

## TERMS OF THE PHILOSOPHICAL ART [I]

# Arguments

Philosophers rarely physically fight, but they do argue: premises are presented, reasoning occurs and conclusions are reached. Arguments are *deductively valid* when conclusions logically follow from premises – when it is impossible for all premises to be true and conclusions false. An argument is *deductively sound*, if it is valid and all the premises are true. An argument may be deductively valid (but not sound) even if premises are false – for example: All women wear hats; Bert is a woman; therefore Bert wears a hat.

Here is an *invalid argument*. If it rains, then the guests get wet; the guests are getting wet; therefore it is raining. It is invalid because even if the premises are true, the conclusion could be false. Perhaps the guests are wet because the host is using a water pistol. There are good arguments that do not pretend to deductive validity, notably inductive ones (see Chapter Eight).

The Feigning Argument has a similarity to our Belle/Tinkers argument. One thing true of my body is that it 'can be feigned by me not to exist', yet that is not true, it seems, of me, of my self. It is not the case that I 'can be feigned by me not to exist'. Hence, I and my body cannot be the identical item; so, it is logically possible that one can exist when the other does not – just as the different locations of Belle and Tinkers shows that it is logically possible that one can exist without the other. Logical possibility, though, does not ensure that something is naturally or practically possible. Maybe, in practice, Tinkers happens to exist only because of Belle's existence: Belle may have given birth to Tinkers and may affect her in many ways. Here are further examples of the logical point. There is no contradiction in the supposition – it is logically possible – that a man runs a mile in two minutes; but it does not follow that in practice it can happen. There is, it seems, no contradiction in an experience machine existing, but it does not follow that technically one could ever be built.

Is the Feigning Argument any good? In more detail, first, does the conclusion follow from the premisses? That is, if – *if*, note – the premisses are true, then are we committed to the truth of the conclusion? If so, then the argument is valid: validity concerns solely the relationship between premisses and conclusion.

Even if an argument is valid, the conclusion may yet be false: a valid argument may validly transport you from false premisses to false conclusions. From the premisses 'All philosophers are beautiful' and 'Socrates was a philosopher' it validly follows that Socrates was beautiful; but that conclusion is false – Socrates apparently was physically ugly – and so one of the premisses must be false: it is false (surprisingly) that all philosophers are beautiful. (Please see the insert above on arguments.)

In assessing our Feigning Argument then, we need not merely to assess whether the argument is valid, but also whether the premisses are true. With validity and true premisses, we have a deductively *sound* argument, an argument which must have a true conclusion.

Returning directly to Descartes' Premiss 1, Descartes' silver tongue has surely shown us that we can feign – pretend – that bodies do not exist. At this stage, it is a distinct question whether bodies really do not exist: we are just talking of what we can pretend. So, we should accept Premiss 1 as true.

Premiss 2 is open to question; after all, I can feign that the world is such that I never existed: once it was true that I did not exist. In response, perhaps I cannot feign that I do not exist at the time of feigning – contrasting with my ability to feign that my body does not exist at the time of my feigning. Maybe, though, my feigning inability manifests merely poor powers of pretence. Indeed, we ought not to be too impressed by Descartes' foundational *cogito*.

After all, even if it is meant somehow to verify itself – in thinking, Descartes must be existing – it does not follow that Descartes cannot doubt it or pretend it is not so. Ply him with sufficient whisky, and he may doubt even the *cogito*.

Let us grant Descartes the benefit of his doubt so to speak: let us accept Premiss 2 as true as well as Premiss 1. We still have the separate question of whether the conclusion follows from the premisses. If it does (and assuming the premisses are true), then we have a sound argument and hence true conclusion. Remember, it is a remarkable conclusion – that human beings are really distinct from their bodies and brains; so they could, in theory, continue to exist despite bodies and brains being annihilated. We are essentially minds, selves or souls: Descartes uses the terms interchangeably. Non-human animals, so it seems for Descartes, lack minds or souls – though that merits challenge. Just because cats, gorillas and dolphins cannot conduct Cartesian reasoning, it does not follow that they lack consciousness forming their essence.

## A metaphysical principle: the Indiscernibility of Identicals

Descartes' argument has the same form as our valid Belle/Tinkers argument. Such arguments rely on a principle brought to the fore by Leibniz, an outstanding mathematician, scientist and philosopher writing soon after Descartes. Leibniz spoke of the Identity of Indiscernibles which, in part, says: if two seemingly distinct items possess all properties in common, then they are not really two; they are one and the same item.

Now, the Identity of Indiscernibles is open to doubt: can we not conceive of the only objects existing in the universe as being two copper spheres, indistinguishable from each other? They would have all their properties and relations in common, yet would be two. The converse of the principle, though – the

Indiscernibility of Identicals, as it may be called – is plausible. We used it with Belle/Tinkers. If Belle and Tinkers are identical, one and the same individual, then they (so to speak) cannot have different properties; they are indiscernible for they are one. If Belle is raven-haired, so must be Tinkers – assuming that they are one and the same individual.

Leibniz's Indiscernibility of Identicals is well and fine – until it is applied to certain types of properties. Unfortunately, one type includes properties such as 'feigning'. The principle fails to hold when properties involve relations concerning psychological states. Here is an example of failure.

Luke admires the virtuous Verity, as he sees her. He knows her only in his philosophy seminars; she comes over as demure, honest and modest. Yes, Luke admires Verity. Luke reads in the newspapers about the gangsters' moll Maxine. Maxine is a pros-titute who rips off clients: she engages in violent criminal activities. The police's identikit pictures of Maxine show her in disguise. Luke holds Maxine in contempt and loathes her; he certainly lacks admiration for such a woman. It could well transpire, though, that Verity and Maxine are one and the same. One person can present in two different ways to Luke such that he unwittingly holds conflicting psychological attitudes towards that one individual. We now relate the point to the Feigning Argument.

The argument deploys psychological states in the ascriptions to 'my body' and to 'I'; so, it is possible that my body and I are one and the same, but presented differently. Hence, the conclusion does not validly follow from the premises: even if the premises are true, the conclusion could be false. If I looked more closely, so to speak, per-haps I could come to see that my body (or just my brain) and I are identical – just as one day Luke may come to see that Verity and Maxine are one and the same. Mind you, we have been glib with the 'just as'. How could I possibly come to see 'from within' that I am physical? That rhetorical question could be Descartes' reply.

## TERMS OF THE PHILOSOPHICAL ART [II]

# *A priori* v. *a posteriori*

Much of what we know we acquire through experiences – of what others tell us, of what we see, hear etc., and remember of such. We know about Plato, maybe who Venezuela's President is, and that it rained yesterday. That is *a posteriori* knowledge: we could not know such facts by reason alone. In contrast, some knowledge *can* be acquired by reason alone: namely, *a priori* knowledge. We can reason, once we possess relevant concepts, that 29 cannot be divided by 3 without remainder, and that a twin was not an only child. In contrast, understanding a president's role and that Venezuela is a country does not enable us to work out who its president is.

# Contingency *v.* necessity

Contingent truths are true, but they might not have been true. Descartes philosophized, but he might not have; he might have gone in for pig-farming instead. There are contingent falsehoods. 'You are not reading these words.' That is false. It might have been true: you might have slept.

In contrast, there are necessary truths and necessary falsehoods. Necessary truths – for example, that $2 + 2 = 4$ – cannot have been otherwise; they hold under all possibilities. Yes, the symbols, '2' etc., might have been used differently; but given current meanings, what is expressed must be true. 'A thousand men cannot undress a naked man' is a necessary truth, known *a priori*. Contradictions are necessary falsehoods: it cannot possibly be true that these words right here are printed *solely* in black yet also not in black.

Although Descartes' argument clearly has problems, what he argues for may yet be the correct picture of things. After all, just because there are bad arguments to show that Hedwig runs faster than Nicolette, it fails to follow that Hedwig is not the faster runner: let us wait for the race. Descartes' understanding of the human being as a combination of two distinct items, mind and body, may be correct even if his particular arguments are dubious; so, we turn to that understanding.

## Ghosts, machines and the stoical sofa

Descartes' dualism is a dualism between what I essentially am (the self) and my body. More easily, I am my mind – for the self, as said, is taken to be the mind. Descartes thinks of the self, the mind, the soul, as a substance, albeit immaterial, without spatial extent or location; so, it is not in the head. It can no more be located in space than can the number seven. According to Descartes, the self can exist independently of everything else – well, except God. Strictly, argues Descartes, there is only one substance for only God is completely independent of everything else. Speaking a little loosely though, minds – and body – are created substances.

Although the dualistic picture offers the mind and body as distinct items, within this mortal coil they interact. The world impinges on us through perceptions – our seeing, hearing, touching *et al.* We impinge on the world through our actions: decisions and desires move the body. When the clock strikes six, vibrations cause changes in my nervous system, causing aural experiences in my mind which cause me ('my mind') to think that it is time for a drink which leads to my decision to head for the tavern; that decision, a psychological event, causes changes in my brain, causing electrical changes in muscles and resultant walking.

The Cartesian picture – the picture derived from Descartes – presents perception as passively mopping up what the world gives us and then our acting in certain ways. Both the perception and the action are far more complicated than this suggests.

Regarding perception, consider the duck/rabbit picture: what we see can flip from duck to rabbit or rabbit to duck, yet the

## INTERACTING WITH THE WORLD

## Perceiving: seeing the duck/rabbit

What we see flips, from duck to rabbit, yet the lines on the paper remain the same. What we see is not determined solely by what is there to be seen.

## Acting: feeding or poisoning the penguins?

When I cast peanuts in the direction of the penguins, what determines what I am doing? Am I feeding the penguins? Am I killing them? Am I simply ridding myself of unwanted nuts? Am I, strictly speaking, just waving my arm and un-clenching my fingers? Answers hang, in part, on what happens in the world, but also on my intentions, deliberations or motivations – but are such psy-chological states and happen-ings based in an immaterial mind, as Descartes argued?

drawing, the lines on paper, remain unchanged. In perception, we often contribute to what is seen; we are not sponges, passively absorbing the external world. of the external world. Regarding action, what we do is partly determined by the world; our action may be that of (unwittingly) poisoning the penguins, not merely feeding them. If the notice tells us not to feed them, are we feeding them on purpose – and with what purpose? Of course, we may not even be intending to feed them; we may just be waving our arms, not realizing that, as a result, we are sprinkling nuts.

According to Descartes, the mind – the Cartesian *ego* – is essentially a conscious item, a thinking thing, where 'thinking' covers all conscious experiencing. It is an enduring item with psychological qualities, abilities and tendencies – with thoughts, intelligence, desires and sensations (though the latter may also essentially involve the body). Indeed, Descartes seemed to think that we can always directly access our thoughts and beliefs; no deeply unconscious thoughts exist in the Cartesian world.

The mind must be distinct from the body, from the brain, for that latter, in contrast, possesses spatial location, shape and size. Just as it is, apparently, absurd to suppose that physical things – lumps of matter such as bicycles, pebbles, oceans – are thinking or desiring, so it is absurd to suppose that a mind exists so many inches above your jaw, or weighs two pounds. On this view, minds and bodies belong to two radically distinct categories. There is a 'real distinction', a distinction in reality.

Minds are not the sort of things that can be spatial; pebbles are not the sort of things that can be conscious. It is not just that pebbles happen not to be conscious; it is, on Descartes' view, a contradiction to propose that they are. The brain, being but another physical thing, also necessarily lacks conscious experiences – though here on earth it is causally involved in generating some. Recall, there is a big difference between saying that Belle and Tinkers are the same person and saying that Tinkers causes changes in Belle. Further, in saying that the mind is essentially conscious, Descartes means that it *cannot* exist without consciousness. Maybe he believes that during sleep and coma we are still conscious, as in dreams, but often forget those experiences.

Gilbert Ryle, a twentieth-century Oxford philosopher, influenced by Wittgenstein, introduced the term 'category mistake'. Descartes, as implied, is saying that it is a category mistake to ascribe physical properties to the mind. Ryle attacked Descartes for committing his own Cartesian category mistake – in treating the mind as a substance, a thing, yet lacking physical properties. Ryle, with deliberate abuse, labelled Descartes' understanding of mind as of a 'ghost in the machine'. According to Ryle, the mind is not a thing at all. True, we do speak of minds and bodies, as if they are distinct. We may, indeed, identify ourselves more with the mind than the body, even though we speak of having a mind just as of having a body. Language can, though, mislead. In Wittgenstein's terms, language bewitches: philosophy should be a battle against the bewitchment.

Allow me to introduce the average butcher. The average butcher has maybe 1.7 children, but individual butchers cannot have 1.7 children. They have whole numbers of children or none at all. It would be bizarre to conclude that, because the average butcher has a property that individual butchers must lack, the average butcher is a special type of butcher – an immaterial thing – causally related to flesh-and-blood butchers. The average butcher is a 'logical construction' out of flesh-and-blood butchers. Now, much of what is true of the mind is not readily true of the brain and body parts, but maybe the mind is a logical construction, a way in which we summarize features of the body and behaviour – an approach discussed in Chapter Six. Here, though, we continue with direct objections to Descartes' dualism.

For Descartes it is a contingent fact – one courtesy of God – that a mind, on Earth, is linked to a human body. The logic of the distinction between mind and body would, in principle, allow for a buttercup to be linked to a human mind, for a digital machine to be so linked – for, indeed, a sofa. Of course, buttercups, machines and sofas are unable to manifest what any such linked minds think and feel – or maybe the sofa's mind is particularly stoical. The absurdity of those apparent logical possibilities should surely make us hesitate before swallowing Cartesian dualism. Let us assume, though, that Descartes' God would rule out such bizarre possibilities. The Cartesian picture still has problems.

We possess a scientific understanding of material things such as metals and marmalade. Further, neuroscientists can increasingly show which parts of the brain are activated, when we perceive, imagine or think – but that may just show that brain activities *cause* thoughts, memories, decisions and so forth, not that they are *identical* with the psychological happenings. Further still, if we turn to psychology, analysts and therapists, there is no body of knowledge, similar to physics or chemistry, concerning what *constitutes* minds, the psychological stuff.

Putting that constitutive question to one side, how can two created substances, mind and body, interact? How can a non-spatial, immaterial something be the cause of the brain's electrochemical activities that cause heavy limbs' movements and vocal chords' production of meaningful sounds?

The interaction problem much exercised Descartes and subsequent philosophers. It led Malebranche, a priest inspired by Descartes, to argue for Occasionalism as a solution: on the *occasion* of your willing your arm to rise, God intervenes and moves your arm appropriately. Now, God is immaterial and non-spatial, as are we, but with God's being all powerful, whatever he wills must happen. That generates moral problems: if you will your arm to rise to stab Caesar, then, because God performs the stabbing, it looks as if God is minimally an accessory to Caesar's murder. Working within the Cartesian metaphysics, Malebranche's stance is not, though, as crazy as it appears. Arguably he is suggesting that causality needs simply to be understood as regularities grounded in nature, albeit, for Malebranche, a divine nature.

The interaction problem is a problem only if causes and their effects must possess certain properties in common, such as both being spatial. Now, minds and bodies exist in time, but in other respects they are understood as essentially different. Let us remind ourselves, though, that in the physical world gravity differs radically from apples yet affects them, leading to their bruising – and ours – when they fall. Electrical currents are very different from resultant wheel movements. We use those thoughts as an excuse to introduce David Hume, deemed 'the great infidel' by Boswell.

Hume's first work, as he noted, fell 'still born from the press', but his stature these days is high, with his 'empiricist' attempt to derive all knowledge from observations of the world, contrasting with Descartes' 'rationalism' which sought to understand fundamental matters solely by reasoning. How would the Humean approach handle Descartes' problem? Well, Hume looks to experience: when one event causes another, all that we experience is one event, then another – for example, the tube is squeezed and toothpaste emerges. There is far more to Hume's analysis than that, as we shall see later – and squeezing is  itself a causal act – but the Humean stance is sufficient to make us question whether effects must have some essential similarity with their causes.

## 'I am not solely as a pilot in a vessel'

Interaction, arguably, presents a non-problem for dualism, but the dualistic understanding of action raises questions. It sees all human *actions* as involving psychological events; in contrast bodily changes, such as kidney functions, involve no psychology, no subject's direct control. The dualistic idea is this: wanting breakfast, I decide to head to the fridge. The decision is a psychological act, an act of will, a *willing*, that causes the relevant neurological changes leading to the muscular movements fridge-wards.

## MODERN PHILOSOPHERS

**Rationalists:** Descartes emphasized reason for gaining knowledge, our ideas being innate. University courses traditionally deem him 'rationalist' in contrast to 'empiricist'. The distinction is coarse; philosophers are not so easily categorized.

**Spinoza** (1632–77), born in Amsterdam, argued that reality possesses a rational necessity; the good life lies in reason. He identified God with nature, supported toleration and was, for his pains, excommunicated by his synagogue. He became a lens grinder, deemed god-intoxicated by some, atheist by others.

**Leibniz** (1646–1716), unlike Spinoza, was worldly, engaged in diplomacy, yet he became trapped as royal librarian in the backwater of Hanover. He discovered the differential calculus independently of Newton, engaged in experiments, yet reasoned that reality consisted of non-spatial unities. He was mocked by Voltaire for judging this world 'the best possible world'.

**Empiricists:** Contrasting with rationalists, certain philosophers stressed experience and empirical research – a stance of **Francis Bacon** (1561–1626), Lord Chancellor of England. Bacon died of pneumonia, experimenting with snow for meat preservation.

Two leading empiricists, influenced by Newton's scientific successes, are **John Locke** (1632–1704) and **David Hume** (1711–1776). Locke saw himself, philosophically, as under-labourer to 'the incomparable Mr Newton'. The splendid Scottish Enlightenment Hume sought to be a Newton of the psychological. 'Empiricist' also covers **George Berkeley** (1685–1753), later Bishop of Cloyne. He argued that reality consists only of souls and their 'ideas'. Idealism – from 'idea', not 'ideal' – is summed: to be is to be perceived or perceive. Berkeley curiously also advocated tar water as a cure for many ills; psychoanalysts have had a field day.

**Immanuel Kant** (1724–1804) is amongst the greatest of philosophers – with Plato and Aristotle. Awoken from dogmatic slumbers by reading Hume, he synthesized rationalism and empiricism. He also analysed jokes. The jokes and analyses augured poorly for his sense of humour – and dinner parties.

There is the immediate worry that if that willing itself is an *act* – something that I do – then, on this approach, it too needs a prior psychological act; thus, we lapse into a regress of decidings or willings, willings without end.

We may wonder why we should assume that every human action involves or is preceded by a mental act. Reflect on your daily actions – making breakfast, running for the train, reading this book – have they all involved acts of will, and how many? 'Ah,' comes a possible reply, 'acts of will are often unconscious.' That is a non-Cartesian reply, for, as mentioned earlier, Descartes' approach lacks the unconscious; and it is a reasonable reply for others, only if they can independently give grounds for the existence of such unconscious acts.

Somehow, though, we can *intentionally* twiddle our toes, be *motivated* to go for a jog – or *decide* to lie down until the jogging thought fades. The following becomes tempting: there really must be psychological events marking the difference between, for example, your leg twitching outside your control and deliberately jiggling your leg. Deliberations, decisions, intentions – they are surely something. That may, though, manifest another category mistake.

Someone, her leg once in plaster but now unplastered, needs to relearn how to walk: she tries to lift her leg – she strains. Such cases can mislead people into thinking that there must be events akin to little tryings, strainings, willings, whenever we deliberately act – yet there is no good reason to believe that is so.

When actions are performed intentionally, on purpose or deliberately, we accept responsibility for them, often providing reasons for what we did. That truth does not imply that certain prior psychological happenings caused the movements. Doubtless there are many neurological happenings involved, but it is a further controversial claim (see Chapter Six) that sense can be made of psychological happenings being identical with neurological happenings. Let us, though, muse more on Descartes' dualism.

The Cartesian dualistic model seeks to show what is distinctive about humans. It is open to a further vital objection, paradoxically one voiced by Descartes. Regarding my relationship with my body, he writes, I am not solely as a pilot in a vessel, a captain of a ship, but am most intimately linked to my body. The observation highlights the experienced unity of the human being rather than its dualistic division. Phantom limb exceptions apart, we can often tell immediately and in a privileged way the location of our limbs, our need for water, and whether our toes have been trodden on. We do not usually investigate these things as a pilot investigates the state of his ship. The sensation of thirst is radically different from knowing intellectually that we are dehydrated.

Descartes himself speaks of the mind being united to the whole of the body, yet he is dragged back to his basic dualism. Indeed, he argues that the mind/body interaction occurs at a particular point, namely, at the brain's pineal gland. Even if that is so – and there is no good reason to think so – it does nothing to resolve the mind/body unity puzzles. It does nothing to explain how a separate non-physical mind can, for example, intrude upon the physical world, if that world can be completely explained by the physical sciences.

So it is, that we lead into the problem of free will – for many, including Descartes, are tempted by the thought that a further distinctive feature of humans is their ability to act freely. Now, what is that free action; what is it to act freely?

# 2

# Are we responsible for what we do?

On the seashore, some boys are lobbing pebbles; they splash loudly when striking the waters of the rock-pools – the pebbles, not the boys. The pebbles spin high in the air, but gravity wins and down they fall. We could project consciousness onto the pebbles; we may grant them the thoughts, 'I'm freely soaring into blue skies, but have decided now to swirl down into cool waters.' That would be, of course, to anthropomorphize the pebbles: pebbles can do no other than what they do, once set in train by the throws of those larking boys.

'Anthropomorphize the pebbles,' we say; but are we humans in any better position than pebbles? Well, with the pebbles, knowing the force of the throws, angles and wind pressures, we could work out when and where they would land – after all we (well others) can explicitly calculate trajectories, places and times of rockets' lunar landings – but human decisions surely involve far greater complexities. Complexity alone, though, is no indicator of free action. As Nietzsche noted, the tumbling of a waterfall's cascading waters manifests vast complexity, yet in principle, arguably, each drop's swirling movements could be predicted, given the known forces of nature – for the movements are all causally determined.

The philosophical perplexity here is how we find room for free will in nature. It takes some credulity to insist that human beings have evolved such that they stand outside the laws of nature, outside the natural world. That insistence would have humans forming, in Spinoza's mocking terms, 'a kingdom within a kingdom'. Spinoza saw God and Nature as one and the same substance; such heresy, as noted earlier, made him unpopular with Christians and his fellow Jews. According to Spinoza, human beings, as with other creatures – and trees, mountains and, no doubt, marmalade – are solely modifications of 'God or Nature', as waves are modifications of the ocean, falling under natural laws, no more able to do otherwise than pebbles in flight.

If people are completely subject to natural laws, then praise and blame, holding people morally responsible, would seem out of place; yet we send some to gaol, others to psychiatric units, and yet others receive awards. Now, punishment, blame and praise, may be used simply as causal inputs to alter individuals' behaviour – to deter criminals or promote the virtuous – just as drugs, therapies and straightjackets, delivered to the psychiatrically disturbed, are designed to alter what they do. However, talk of what people *morally deserve*, because of their actions, is misplaced, when the individuals are compelled to act as they do or when they could not have done otherwise as implied by the deterministic picture. There is a slogan, from Immanuel Kant, that 'ought' implies 'can': if people cannot act otherwise, then they should not be held morally responsible.

Let us look at the importance we give to free will – and then how it may stand with the deterministic picture sketched.

## Jack, Jill – and kicking the bucket

Consider Jill who knocks over the bucket of water which rolls down the hill, hitting Jack, with death resulting. Jill is causally responsible for his death – had she not knocked the bucket, it would not have rolled and Jack would be an alive and well Jack-the-Lad. Is Jill, though, morally responsible? Does she merit blame (or indeed praise)? Well, she may rightly evade moral responsibility in various ways. She may have tripped because she was startled or was pushed; she did not, so to speak, kick the bucket – it was no intentional action – but a movement caused by external factors, as a tree may fall because of storms. She could not have done otherwise, given those external causes impinging upon her.

Here is another excusing scenario. Jill had no desire to kill Jack, but there was a gun at her head; she had either to aim the bucket at Jack or be shot dead. Even when there is a free choice, moral responsibility is affected by the alternatives available. Indeed, suppose that she wanted to kill Jack, yet it was the trip or push that led to the killing: she is then not morally responsible for that killing, despite her questionable wants. Had it, though, been her desire to kill Jack by the kick-of-bucket method that led to his death, she is then morally responsible – though even now, we may add, 'assuming she could have done otherwise and could have resisted that deathly desire and kicking impulse that caused Jack's demise'.

The importance and problem of free will are hence easily seen – and the 'free will' may cover here, until distinctions are required, 'free decision, choice and action'. On many occasions, we have to decide what to do and, it seems, we have various alternatives between which to choose. Whatever we choose, the apparent free-will requirement is that we could have done otherwise in those same circumstances. The existence of alternatives, of 'could have done otherwise', pins the moral responsibility on us, with mitigations afforded, as mentioned with Jill. Thus we may speak of our action being freely performed, because it resulted from our free choice, free decision – our free will. If our choices, though, are as causally determined as the movements of the pebbles, waterfalls and planets, then the 'could have done otherwise' feature is illusory.

# Determinism, Indeterminism and Free Will

Here is the deterministic picture, from Pierre-Simon Laplace, a French scientist and mathematician writing in 1814:

> We ought to regard the present state of the universe as the effect of its antecedent state and the cause of the state that is to follow. An intelligence, knowing at a given instant all things of which the universe consists, would be able to comprehend the actions of the largest bodies of the world and those of the lightest atoms in one single formula, provided his intellect were sufficiently powerful to subject all data to analysis... The human mind in the perfection it has been able to give astronomy affords a feeble outline of such an intelligence.

That deterministic picture is taken to include human beings. We saw in the previous chapter some problems with treating the mind, the self, as distinct from the human body. It is natural to be drawn towards treating a person as at heart a unity, a biological blob. Of course, the biological blobs that are persons, in contrast to trees, moss and rainforests, have psychological properties; and, in contrast to yaks and sloths, herons and herrings, the biological blobs that are persons can conceptualize differences between appearances and reality; they can, for example, conduct thought experiments about experience machines.

Human beings are part of the seemingly deterministic natural world. In modern garb, human beings have at least some genetic dispositions to behave in certain ways; such dispositions are, though, merely particular features of the causal soup that fixes what we decide and do. Your neural structures and upbringing – your nature and nurture – developed outside your control. If that picture is accurate, then there are causal chains, going back to the primeval slime, to the Big Bang (or whatever is the preferred cosmological speculation), which, over billions of years, led to the solar systems which generated conditions whereby evolution occurred, leading to you and me and our neurological networks – and some resultant pebble throwing and philosophical writings and readings.

In the deterministic picture, the world is taken to operate according to certain laws of nature, regularities or causal relations. Typically, given those laws and the circumstances – the initial conditions – the events that then occur do so with a natural necessity. Natural necessity? Well, scientific determinism is not committed to a logical determinism. Scientific determinism accepts that we may logically conceive of the pebble – that is, without contradiction – instead of splashing down, flying off to the moon, perhaps even sprouting angelic wings; however, the causal world that we inhabit is not one of pebbles winging off to moons. Because of gravity, pebbles accelerate downward at 32 feet per second per second, and cannot naturally do otherwise, even though there is no logical contradiction in supposing otherwise. In this world as it is, spilt milk fails to clamber back into bottles and regular human beings cannot cause the seas to part with waves of hands.

Newton said, 'I can calculate the movement of the stars, but not the madness of men.' Determinism, though, does not rely upon anyone's ability to calculate or predict future events; it simply relies on the fact that the events will occur, given natural laws and initial conditions. Determinism need not be a psychological determinism, one that claims, for example, that our actions are always determined by perceived self-interest. We may briefly wonder about evidence for that psychological determinism – often held – and spot its error, before returning to free will.

You engage in an activity – gardening, helping the poor, supporting your library. You say that you like gardening, that you ought to help the poor, that you want to improve the library.

The mistaken response is that therefore you are acting for your own sake: to gain the blossoming delights, avoid pangs of guilt, and satisfy your wants. Ultimately, you always pursue your own self-interest, as you think of it. The conclusion is that actions are never truly altruistic, motivated by the interests of others. That conclusion is as mistaken as saying that because our genes are metaphorically selfish, therefore we are selfish. Let us develop the point.

It can be an interesting empirical hypothesis that all actions are motivated by perceived self-interest, yet it has to face (seeming) counterevidence: on occasions people appear motivated solely by the interests of others. Arguably, it is only because of prior commitment to the theory 'everyone always acts selfishly' that any selflessness is taken as mere appearance – that the mother running into the burning house to save her child is 'really' motivated by self-interest, to avoid feelings of guilt or condemnation by others. If you follow that line, you are simply defining altruism out of existence: you are not discovering, through empirical research, that it does not exist. If you follow that line, you will need to regenerate the former distinction between the selfless and the selfish; pithily put, you will tend to prefer individuals who 'selfishly' act for free over those who 'selfishly' act for a fee.

Returning to free will and the deterministic world, where neurological events cause our decisions and actions, a plausible requirement for acting freely, as said, is to possess the ability to do otherwise than we do. That seems incompatible with a deterministic world. With greater accuracy, the incompatibility exists if the free-will demand is that you could have chosen otherwise than you did, despite the circumstances being otherwise exactly the same. Of course, in a deterministic world, you could well have chosen differently, had the circumstances been different – for they may then have causally affected you differently.

# FATALISMS

Universal scientific determinism claims that all events, including human actions, result from prior events and laws of nature. Even if quantum's indeterminacy holds, nature is deterministically firm when not sub-atomic. Such determinism differs from other challenges to free will.

**Fatalism (hard)** claims that, *whatever you do*, certain events will happen. That is obviously true concerning planetary movements: whatever you do, their movements remain unaltered. Fatalists, though, may look into the future and tell you it is fated that you will die tomorrow from a scorpion's sting – whatever you do, whether you go to the zoo, visit your aunt, or stay in bed.

**Fatalism (soft)**, in contrast, may insist that it is fated that you will die tomorrow at noon, but *not whatever you do*. In fact, if you go to the zoo tomorrow, you will be fine; but – maybe because of the prediction – you decide to stay in bed and there you indeed meet your death through an escaped scorpion's unwelcome visitation.

**The Lazy Argument**, from antiquity, is little more than the empty sigh: 'What will be, will be.' True, what will be, will be; but it does not follow that what will be, *must* be. Often what will be depends upon choices. The Lazy Argument says that it is silly to revise for the test. You will either pass or not – so why bother to revise? The argument ignores how revision may be key to your test success – or failure.

**The Truth Argument** starts thus: thousands of years ago, it was true then that you would now be reading this book, even though no one knew it. So, it seems, you are reading this book of logical necessity. It would also be logically necessary that you are not now reading this book, had the truth years ago been that you would not. Either way, given the necessity, you could not have done otherwise.

The argument assumes that truths exist in time. Even if that is so, it merits challenge. From the truth years ago that you will be reading today, it necessarily follows that you will be reading today; but it does not necessarily follow that you will be of necessity.

Free will is a puzzle, readily granted, if the world is deterministic: the causes upon us are taken as compulsions. Here we should
reintroduce Hume on causation, touched upon in the previous
chapter. In our common sense thinking, causes may be viewed as
'compelling' some effects to follow, but Hume draws us away
from that thinking. Here is an illustration:

> Lighting a match with certain gases present caused the explo-
> sion. One event is followed by another, and, we may be inclined
> to accept, other events of the match-lighting type with relevant
> gases present are also followed by explosive events. We could
> add that usually, had such match lighting not occurred, those
> explosions of that type would not have occurred.

There are many complexities and caveats raised by the above
Humean analysis, but his approach should dispel the thought that
there is a metaphysical necessity that glues effects to causes.
Scientific explanations somewhere conclude with 'this is what
happens: when events of that type occur, events of this type
occur'. Arguably, in the end, we rest content with brute regularities. Those brute regularities, though, may yet still strike us as
undermining our being able to have acted otherwise in the same
circumstances.

Now, some readers may be agitating for the indeterminism, the
randomness, of quantum theory. That theory is often perceived
as wiping out, as old-fashioned, deterministic mechanism.
Theories concerning the quantum level may, of course, be
transient – who knows? Even if indeterminacy holds, though, it
provides no solution to the free-will puzzle for, at the macro
level, deterministic laws, probabilistic or not, remain firm.
Whatever the meanderings of sub-atomic particles, water boils
and human beings currently cannot fly unaided.

Even if our 'free will' choices and decisions occur at the
brain's sub-atomic quantum level and are the source of the more

familiar neurological changes that cause people, for example, to speak of freely choosing to visit Paris, that sub-atomic source fails to establish the visit as freely made. True, the choice, if random, could have been different; but a free choice is not usually under-stood as random. Particles randomly moving, even if conscious, are not thereby acting freely. Choices, decisions, actions randomly produced, disconnected from desires, character and beliefs are those more distinctive of the insane than of individuals acting freely.

## Revising 'free will': Casanova Casper

Despite the allure of 'could have done otherwise', it may be a misunderstanding of our concerns about free will, choice and action. Perhaps there is an understanding of 'free will' that makes sense, be the world deterministic or no.

You decide to move to Paris. No one forces you. You want to make the move; you have excellent reasons. You love the French cuisine; a wonderful job offer has come your way – and your lover is Parisian. So, you move there freely. Is the move free only because you could have done otherwise? Despite your delight in the cuisine, the job, the lover, what is important for free will is that, in those very circumstances, you could have stayed put in London. Suppose you stayed put: would that manifest an individual acting freely? It would be bizarre behav-iour, maybe requiring causal explanation. Or perhaps further reasons could be entered – such as a passion to make a philo-sophical point.

In contrast to the 'could have done otherwise' approach, we often see ourselves as free agents when possessing reasons, sometimes overwhelming reasons, for our actions. With a para-doxical lilt, we may even be inclined to say 'I could do no other' or, 'I was determined to do that'. Martin Luther of the Protestant

Reformation was in control of himself when he allegedly announced, 'Here I stand; I can do no other.'

Taking a cue from the above, acting freely is misunderstood if requiring 'could have done otherwise', for it is suggestive of indifference. Indeed, 'liberty of indifference' is a dismissive Humean term for that understanding of free will. If free will is being able to do otherwise in exactly the same circumstances, then it looks as if what is valued is the possibility of choices being utterly detached from circumstances, reasons, motivations for actual choices – as if the agents are indifferent, uncaring, about outcomes.

Taking a further cue from the Parisian tale, maybe the criterion for people acting freely is their doing what they want to do, manifesting, in Hume's expression, a 'liberty of spontaneity'. That criterion offers a compatibilist solution to the free will problem, 'compatibilist' because a deterministic world is compatible with your sometimes doing what you want and getting what you want. The causal deterministic chains may be such that when you want to take a shower, you take a shower; nothing within or without impedes satisfaction of that want. Your wants, though, can come into conflict, so the criterion suggested needs refinement. The following demonstrates the need.

Casper, a Casanova type, delights in wine, women and song – well, not necessarily the song. He loves flirting with ladies of allure, and, when in flirtatious intoxication, he is doing what he wants and often gets what he wants. Yet our Casper, unlike the historic Casanova, would love not to be such a man; he would love instead to spend his time in philosophical pursuits, reading Plato. Although philosophy and seduction are far from incompatible, the excessive time Casper spends on seduction rules out time for philosophy. Casper possesses a second-order desire, a desire about desires: he desires not to have the first order desires for constant repetitive seduction. Thus, since our Casper identifies with the second-order desire, he is lacking control and not getting what he truly wants; he is as much at the mercy of his first-order seductive desires as he would be at the mercy of external gunmen ordering him to hand over cash.

Contrast Casper with a wanton – an individual who recognizes no continuing clash of desires, but whose actions are always the overall outcome of immediate desires. Most non-human animals arguably are wantons – as are certain unthinking humans swept by rowdy emotions, lusts and drives.

Such examples glide us towards autonomy – towards being self-governing such that it is we who are making the decisions, uncompelled by forces outside: we are the source of our choices. Thus it is that some philosophers have spoken of higher and lower selves. Of course, talk of one person possessing selves is highly misleading. Further, the 'higher' may suggest that the second-order desires are necessarily morally superior to the first – but that is easily challenged. We may conceive of a timid young woman who desires to stay at home studying, bettering herself – perhaps her basic character was formed by conservative, puritanical parents – yet she would also love not to be such a person, but a rebel. Her second-order 'higher' desire is for her to overcome those first-order studious desires, enabling her to rock through a life of degeneracy, promiscuity and rebellion – arguably not at all morally desirable.

Autonomy quickly raises political concerns. One society may promote freedom for its citizens by not imposing external obstacles on behaviour, save to prevent harm to others; another society, though, may impose obstacles as an aid to its citizens in overcoming obstacles internal to themselves, thus becoming self-governing, doing what they truly want. Here comes a classic example.

Many smokers want to abandon smoking, yet cigarettes are readily available and they succumb; so external obstacles, by way of disincentives, are introduced. Those smokers suffer some external restrictions on their smoking habits, restrictions that help them to achieve what they truly want – in this case, to overcome their first-order smoking desires. Of course, those smokers who have no desire to give up smoking may find themselves oppressed by the anti-smoking laws and ethos.

In Homer's *Odyssey*, we find Odysseus wanting to hear the Sirens' song without being lured to a watery grave; so he bade his sailors bind him to the mast and block their ears, ensuring that they would be deaf both to the song and to his later demands for release when lured by the Sirens' sensuous singing ways.

In such cases, people's 'negative' liberty – manifested by available opportunities – is curtailed in order to promote autonomy, their 'positive' liberty, of getting what they 'truly' want. The terms 'liberty' and 'freedom', are used interchangably here.

Dangers, stressed by Isaiah Berlin in the mid-twentieth century, arise when governments, imams, bishops and other authorities claim to know what their people truly want – what is in their best interests – even though the people may see their best interests otherwise. A totalitarian regime may repress its people, intruding into their private lives – perhaps with regard to free speech, religion and sexual expression – sincerely maintaining that it is doing what is best for all and sundry. The regime may, in Rousseau's paradoxical words, 'force people to be free', insisting that, despite protestations, the individuals really are free. They possess positive freedom, their true interests secured; it is just that they fail to appreciate that that is so. Beware such reasoning.

Even when negative liberty is extensive – when the law permits all manner of activities – your *effective* liberty may yet be small. In many societies, people are at liberty to own yachts, eat in expensive restaurants and seek private education. Such negative liberty is, though, a charade for most people; it is no effective freedom because to make use of those opportunities you need significant money – which you may well lack. You also need certain desires and character – to which we turn, shuffling a little further into political philosophy.

# Luck

Contemporary politicians readily promote fairness in terms of 'equal opportunities', equal freedoms. They worry, for example, when the poor do worse educationally than others, that the poor have been unfairly treated. Compensation – additional educational help, easier university admission – is therefore justified. True, the concerned wealthy may give only lip-service to equal opportunities: in practice, they seek advantages for their offspring through expensive tuition, trips abroad and inheritances. We pop such inconsistencies to one side

Many lives go badly, with resultant inequalities and unfairness. They sometimes do so through laziness or talents squandered. The standard response is that individuals with such characteristics have only themselves to blame, yet it is far from clear why those individuals should be treated as more responsible for their characteristics than those born blind are for their blindness. If the blind merit assistance, then ought not the feckless and reckless – for have they not been unlucky with their character traits?

The question arising is whether the state should seek to ensure that people develop worthwhile wants and character, helping to make them autonomous. Paternalistic interference merits no principled moral outrage. As already seen, most of us – without going as far as Rousseau – accept that some wants should be altered. We seek to train children, for their own benefit, to prefer good food over junk, to value education over watching violent films. Laws and ethos discourage smoking and promote exercise. The puzzle – as so often is the case – is where to draw lines; it seems we have to muddle through.

Political interest in equal opportunities, it is worth noting, often leads to the thought that something has gone wrong when there are 'on average' differences between specified groups of people – for example, when girls do better at school than boys;

when company directors and engineers are more likely to be male than female; when high status universities have proportionately more private 'public' school educated than state school entrants. Yet just because there exist such inequalities, it does not follow that they are unjustified, requiring correction. They need to be considered case by case, with assessment of the inequality causes and what, if anything, is wrong about them. It is no self-evident truth – in some cases no truth at all – that males and females ought to be equally distributed with respect to illnesses, sports, occupations and theatre attendances.

We must, though, edge our way back to the underlying metaphysical puzzles here. Consider the provision of flutes and flute lessons. Simply providing equal flute resources to all, without further ado, is silly: some lack flute aptitude or interest, whereas a few show great flautist potential. Yet, as well as helping those talented and motivated, perhaps the state, through biological intervention – genetic changes – should assist others to acquire flute-playing talents, motivation and flautist delight. Try the following thought experiment:

> Occupation pills are available, generating occupational talents. By appropriate pill popping, individuals can become talented flautists, footballers or philosophers – good at tilling the soil, maintaining sewers or working on factory lines. The state engineers that we pop such pills. Maybe who receives which is determined by fair lotteries. In contrast to current practices, greater financial rewards go to those with the less desirable jobs. In fact, perhaps pills are developed to ensure people are happy with their lot, in their occupation, their station and its duties.

The speculation leads us to wonder quite what the self is – the autonomous self. Whether through state intervention, pill-popping or just regular nature and nurturing, your character, your different desires, your identification with some and not others, all result from causes over which you had no say, no control. They all ultimately result from luck – good or bad.

To be freed from luck would seem impossible. It is impossible for, if we remove everything about ourselves that is not of our own making, there is nothing left of us.

The reference to nothing – our being no *thing* – is taken seriously by Jean-Paul Sartre, the French chain-smoking existentialist. Sartre valuably reminds us – and the idea derives from Kant – that, whatever the evolutionary and cultural tales concerning nature and nurture, we cannot escape making choices: we must treat ourselves at least *as if* free. Even if convinced of determinism's truth, we still need to decide whether to put on the red dress or the blue – go to the gym or read an improving book. Yes, we may seek advice; but we still must decide whether to take the advice proffered.

## Human that we are

We need to treat ourselves as free – and so too others. Our relationships generate feelings such as anger, love and remorse; admiration, indignation and forgiveness. We cannot live human lives without such attitudes, such 'reactive attitudes', towards others. Dostoyevsky asks, regarding a criminal, what can I do if I don't feel resentment? If we see another as subject to laws of nature, the object of resentment 'vanishes into thin air, its reasons evaporate, the offender nowhere to be found, the affront ceases to be an offence… something like toothache, for which none is to blame'.

The norm is to treat human beings as moral agents, responsible for what they do. Exceptionally, in contrast, the objectifying attitude gains a foothold, when, for example, others are rocked from emotional storms within and so, out of control. The puzzle

## EXISTENTIALISM

Existentialism covers a range of philosophers and artists, many of whom were unaware of the term. Philosophers tend to fall under the existentialist label if they focus on the singularity and uniqueness of each human being, rather than searching for common human qualities or 'the' way of life. They may stress the anguish, the anxiety, of human existence, through the need to make choices, to treat ourselves as free in the values we espouse.

**Jean-Paul Sartre** (1905–1980) most famously embraced the existentialist label, together with his long-standing associate Simone de Beauvoir (1908–1986). Sartre was influenced by Heidegger. Sartre's slogan is that for a human – for the *pour soi*, the being-for-itself – 'existence precedes essence'. That is, human beings are not things with a fixed essence, such as are trees and spoons. Human consciousness is nothingness, a *no*-thing-ness. 'Man makes himself' through his choices. It is bad faith – *mauvaise foi* – if we view ourselves as something settled, as if we must be a certain sort of person or must follow someone's orders.

**Søren Kierkegaard** (1813–1855) is seen as an early existentialist. In contrast to the atheist Sartre, he was Christian; Christianity mysteriously combines the temporal and eternal. He too emphasizes the need for individuals to take responsibility for their actions. 'Life,' he writes, 'must be lived forwards, though can only be understood backwards.' Kierkegaard highlights choices as leaps, to show that intellectual reflection is insufficient for action. Religious belief, taking us beyond both the instant delights of the aesthetic and the eternal rules of morality, demands a leap of faith.

**Friedrich Nietzsche** (1844–1900) is most famously associated with 'God is dead'. Values themselves require evaluation. Christian values weigh us down with pity, argues Nietzsche. Values that breed resentment, envy and cowardice need rejection. Individuals must choose their own values – hence, his eternal recurrence thought experiment that we meet at the end of this book's Epilogue.

of responsibility, though, resurfaces: if the non-responsibility card is properly played in some cases to excuse behaviour – 'she is mentally ill; he was not himself' – it seems it needs playing everywhere. When murderous thugs plead innocence because they are not to blame for their genetic make-up and upbringing, judges may, by way of reply, justify life sentences of hard labour – for the judges too lacked control over their genes, upbringing and desires to place murderers behind bars.

In practice, we tend to blame and praise when those attitudes can alter the recipients' behaviour; in practice, that sets the boundaries of the person, the moral agent. There is little point in berating Jill for kicking the bucket and causing Jack's death, if she tripped – save to encourage her to be more careful. There is a point in blaming her, punishing her, if she deliberately sought the death – for that may affect her future deliberations and certainly, when behind bars, also her behaviour. That approach, though, as highlighted earlier, is to understand praise and blame solely in terms of their utility in generating beneficial consequences – and that smacks of treating people as objects for manipulation, in tension with the reactive attitudes that we must live by.

♈

Our reflections lead to an apparent unsatisfactory conclusion – that we have to live by an illusion, an illusion of free will; the concept of free will must, it seems, be vacuous or self-contradictory for it can have application neither in a completely deterministic world nor in one with indeterminism present. Indeed, even compatibilist attempts at solution appear to lead us into the nonsensical requirement that the self be nothing at all. Matters may become even worse for, if scientific determinism holds, then all the reasoning steps we make about free will and determinism must, in some way, be chains of causes and effects; but such causal sequences are no respecters of validity and good reasoning. Yes, if all men are mortal and Socrates is a man, then it logically must follow that Socrates is mortal; but what goes on in our neurology such that the causal relations between our neural states match those logical relations?

And in all of the above, we have struggled with the elusive I, with what is the subject, if there is one, which feels itself free. Time, then, to approach these intermeshed puzzles from the question of what survives when we survive through time, when we look forward to futures and remember the past. Time, then, to muse upon what constitutes, as the seasons change, our persisting as the same individuals, albeit much ravaged by those seasons rolling on – by the years that pass by, in some cases leading to wisdom, patience and autumn mellowness, in other cases generating but wrinkles, irritability and memory loss.

# 3

# Surviving

You wake up. You know who you are. 'It's me again,' you could be tempted into saying, as you peer in the mirror, surprised at how bright you look so early in the morning – or saddened by yet another grey hair or added flabbiness. Despite such changes, you regularly have no doubt who you are – and no doubt that it is still you who went to bed the night before and who, many years ago, owned a guinea pig, argued with teachers and wanted to change the world. You have, over the years, undergone huge changes: think how different your body, attitudes and beliefs are from when you were a child; reflect on how you must have forgotten many events, yet now – with luck – know so much more about life. Those changes are examples of two broad, yet changing continuities, the physical and the psychological. Yet is there – must there be – something more than such continuities?

The question we are broaching is: what makes you the same person, the same self, over time – your 'diachronic' identity? It is the philosophical topic of 'personal identity'. Here threatens terminological confusion, for I may persist, despite personality alterations: 'I am a different person,' I may metaphorically murmur, while recognizing that it is still the same I, with the same memories, same bodily continuity. The topic herewith is really what constitutes the self's persistence, a *metaphysical* question. Note that the question differs from the *epistemic* question of how we can tell whether, for example, we are speaking to the same person as last week. The way we tell may typically be by bodily continuity – by fingerprints or DNA – yet what constitutes someone being the identical individual over time may not require having the same body.

If tomorrow, next year, the next decade, I still exist, the tempting thought can be that there must be something – an enduring thing – that persists throughout that time. In Chapter One, we met Descartes' claim that the self, the denotation of 'I', is an immaterial persisting substance. Religious belief often offers such an entity, the soul, as what constitutes the persisting self – the soul being immune from physical decay, with potential for eternal life. The offer, though, is no obvious help in determining what makes me, me, for the nature of a soul is as mysterious as what makes me me. Souls, indeed, are said not to be in space; so, we may wonder just what could individuate them, making them distinct selves, rather than a single self or world soul, with a myriad of conflicting experiences

## 'I go with the psychology'

Two broad approaches to personal identity have been mentioned: the physical and the psychological. The seventeenth-century John Locke brought to prominence some thought experiments designed to show that the psychological is key. Here is a Lockean thought experiment:

> For should the soul of a prince, carrying with it the consciousness of the prince's past life, enter and inform the body of a cobbler, as soon as deserted by his own soul, everyone sees he would be the same person with the prince, accountable only for the prince's actions.

Whether there is an enduring something, a soul or substance, beneath our psychological states and occurrences – and arguably Locke thought there was – it is, he maintains, irrelevant regarding our personal identity. That identity of a person exists through his consciousness and:

> as far as this consciousness can be extended backwards to any past action or thought, so far reaches the identity of that person: it is the same self now it was then, and it is by the same self with this present one that now reflects on it, that that action was done.

Locke thus separates the continuity of the man, the biological body, from the continuity of the *person*, of what makes me me.

It needs to be stressed that 'person' is a forensic concept for Locke, that is, one which locates who is the continuing individual to be held responsible for past deeds. A necessary and sufficient condition for your being the same person as that individual ten years ago who broke the Bank of Monte Carlo is that your memory stretches back to your committing the deed. If you can remember it 'from within' as your deed, then that is sufficient for your identity with that agent so many years ago; if you cannot so remember, then you are not that identical agent, memory being also a necessary condition for sameness of person. That clearly has consequences for punishment, for blame and praise. If, because of memory loss, you are not the same person as the war criminal, even though you are the same biological entity, the same man, then punishment meted out to you is unjust for it is meted out to the wrong person.

The focus on consciousness as maintaining me as me generates not merely moral and legal surprises, such as the above, but also logical difficulties. Here is a classic difficulty, from the eighteenth century 'common sense' Scottish philosopher, Thomas Reid:

> Suppose a brave officer to have been flogged as a boy for robbing an orchard, to have taken a standard from the enemy in his

## PERSONAL IDENTITY: BEFORE AND AFTER LOCKE

**Spinoza**: Locke, writing in the 1690's, is often credited with introducing the problem of personal identity into philosophy, but here is Spinoza's *Ethics*, published posthumously in 1677:

> Sometimes a man goes through such changes that it would be hard to maintain that he remained the same man. I have heard stories about a Spanish poet who suffered an illness after which he had so completely forgotten his past life that he didn't believe that his stories and tragedies were his own work. If he had also forgotten his native language, he could easily have been thought a grown-up infant.

Spinoza argues that an elderly man believes an infant's nature to be so different from his own that he would be unpersuaded he ever was an infant, had he not witnessed examples of the infancy of others. Probably Spinoza understands one's persistence as residing in memory continuity – as later found in Locke.

**Hume**: Locke's philosophy retained vestiges of the existence of underlying substances. Hume, a more thoroughgoing empiricist, clears them away and also the 'identity' in personal identity:

> When I turn my reflection on myself, I never can perceive this self without some one or more perceptions; nor can I ever perceive any thing but the perceptions. 'Tis the composition of these, therefore, which forms the self... Suppose the mind to be reduc'd even below the life of an oyster. Suppose it to have only one perception, as of thirst or hunger... Do you conceive any thing but merely that perception? Have you any notion of self or substance?

At best, the self is a 'bundle of perceptions' – of experiences, thoughts, memories, intentions. Hume likens the mind to a theatre: only successive perceptions constitute the mind. We have no notion 'of the place where these scenes are represented, or the materials of which it is composed'. The theatre metaphor must not mislead. There is no self, surveying the scenes.

first campaign, and have been major general in advanced life; suppose, also, that when taking the standard, he was conscious of his having been flogged, and that, when made general, he was conscious of his taking the standard, but had lost consciousness of his flogging. These things being supposed, it follows from Mr Locke's doctrine, that he who was flogged is the same person who took the standard, and that he who took the standard is the same person who became general. Whence it follows, if there be any truth in logic, that the general is the same person with him who was flogged. But the general's consciousness does not reach so far back as his flogging; therefore, according to Mr Locke's doctrine, he is not the person who was flogged. The general is, and at the same time is not, the same person with him who was flogged at school.

Reid's fine challenge hits home because of Locke's commitment to identity, a transitive relation. If A is identical with B and B is identical with C, then A is identical with C. Contrast that transitive relation with a non-transitive relation such as 'loves'. If Aimee loves Bill and Bill loves Candy, it certainly does not follow that Aimee loves Candy.

Many philosophers, in the spirit of Locke, and even more so in that of Hume, conceive of the identity of a self as not true identity, but a continuity of overlapping, causally related thoughts, intentions and memories, some more vivid than others, some fading, some vanishing. Because I continue to speak of 'I' throughout, I may wrongly conclude that there must be a single thread running throughout; but that is as mistaken as believing that a strong rope requires at least one single thread from beginning to end. What seems essential is the overlapping. You may be unable to remember your deeds as a child, but you can remember those as a teenager, and when a teenager, those as a child. Your identity is a matter of psychological continuity and is not proper identity. Mind you, the approach needs caveats: I may recall deeds last year, but none of yesterday's.

The above approach fits well with the feeling that those in persistent vegetative states are dead – that the biological shells live on, yet they, the persons, are no more. It does not fit well with the thought that I may continue to exist, even if I undergo radical discontinuity in my experiences or, because of Alzheimer's, end up with no psychological continuity with a past at all. To make this more vivid, consider the following – yes, another thought experiment – as 'Perspective One'.

## Sadistic surgeons

Ben and Belinda are trapped, awaiting speculative surgery. The background is that, with supposed increased neurological understanding, surgeons can replace decaying brain cells. Before they do so, while the patient is under anaesthetic, they often 'copy over' the patient's neurological patterns, firings – perhaps onto hard drives – then they perform the cell replacements after which they copy back the patterns onto the refreshed brain. The patient awakes, being still the same person, with memories, projects and character the same. The assumption is that psychological states are grounded in neurological patterns; after all, in everyday life, cells of the brain can be replaced: atoms and subatomic particles come and go. Of course, we may wonder whether the scenario in detail makes sense. Perhaps it does; let us pretend so.

Ben and Belinda will be placed under anaesthetic; their neurological patterns – and hence their memories, projects, beliefs, character – will be interchanged. On waking, the Ben-body, so to speak, will have Belinda's psychological states and the Belinda-body will have Ben's. Coming forth post-operatively from the Ben-body will be observations such as, 'Yes, I am Belinda, I have all my usual memories, I still plan to study philosophy, though it feels odd to have this deep Ben voice and what a pity no one warned me about Ben's twitch and missing leg.'

Here comes the point of this thought experiment. Suppose you are Belinda, waiting before the operation, and you are truthfully told by the sadistic surgeons that after the operation, they are going to torture one of the resulting people and set free the other, granted considerable wealth. You are no masochist; you love money. Choosing purely self-interestedly, would you prefer the money to go to the Ben-body or the Belinda-body?

The temptation is surely to see yourself as going where the psychology goes and hence, if you are Belinda, to encourage the surgeons to give the post-operative wealth to the Ben-body. After all, when the Ben-body awakes, the person there will remember being Belinda, living her life 'from within', will remember recommending wealth, not torture, for the Ben-body, and will be pleased if the surgeons have followed her pre-operative recommendation.

The above Perspective One thought experiment may be approached very differently – as Perspective Two. Forget about Ben and the details above for the moment. You are Belinda, captured by sadistic surgeons; they will torture you tomorrow. You do not welcome the morrow. It will be you being tortured – horrendous, painful, deeply unwanted. They spy your fearful anticipation; they make a concession. Before torturing you, they will wipe your memories (apart from general knowledge of language and life); after all, you do forget things, so it would be no difficult thing to cause you radical memory loss. Hence, just before the torture begins, you will be saying things such as 'I've no idea who I am.' You should still fear the future torture of this Belinda-body, even though all psychological continuity distinctive of you has been erased.

Some additions to this Perspective Two tale easily transform it into the original Perspective One, yet, in contrast with that perspective, you continue to urge no torture to this Belinda-body. If you are told that, after wiping your memories and so forth, a different set will be imposed on your brain – the Ben set – you may still fear the torture: why should having mistaken memories, changed intentions *et al* make you, this biological entity, suffer any the less? And why would you feel that you will not be suffering when this Belinda-body is tortured, if you learn that your memories and intentions will not be wiped for good, but will be copied onto a Ben brain?

The two perspectives above reveal the following dilemma. You certainly do not look forward to any torture. Should you hope that tomorrow this current body is not tortured, whatever its psychological states – or should you hope that tomorrow whichever body carries these current psychological states of yours should not be tortured?

The line of thought in Perspective Two suggests the bodily criterion for your identity – continuity of body, hence continuity of you – yet it seems possible to exist with a different body: recall the earlier Lockean possibility. Kafka's *Metamorphosis* tells the tale of Gregor Samsa who awakes one morning from uneasy dreams and finds himself transformed into an insect. 'What has happened to me?' he asks. We are lulled into Samsa being identified by his psychology; yet the evidence provided by such a tale could lead us to describe the situation as one in which a gigantic insect suddenly has false memories of being Gregor Samsa.

A general problem with using the psychological criterion for personal identity is that it permits replication: your identity becomes analogous to software that may be played on different hardware. There could hence be a thousand 'you's; yet that is nonsense. There could be a thousand copies of you, but that is not the same as a thousand 'you's.

Our natural belief – for what it is worth – is that you and I are biological entities, animals with consciousness. If the animal persists, yet the consciousness (in some brain story) flies off elsewhere, how can it be judged which you are?

# Identity disposal

People can survive, even if one brain hemisphere is destroyed. True, they will usually be paralysed down one side – and if the left hemisphere is destroyed they typically lack speech – but so long as one hemisphere is undamaged, they continue as themselves, albeit with extreme paralysis and related losses. Assuming that is indeed true, let us deploy a further thought experiment. You are placed under anaesthetic and your brain is divided, the left hemisphere being popped inside and appropriately connected to a new previously brainless body, Lefty, and the right hemisphere similarly into a different new body, Righty. Lefty and Righty awake, with partial but different paralyses. Where are you?

If you can still exist as you with just one hemisphere working, then you should be Lefty. Equally so, you should be Righty. Now, recalling the transitivity of identity, as you are identical with Lefty and identical with Righty, Lefty is identical with Righty. You are both Righty and Lefty. That feels counterintuitive. Lefty has your memories and so forth; Righty has your memories and so forth. However, when they look at each other they do not understand themselves as one and the same person. Lefty knows neither how things look from Righty's viewpoint nor Righty's current thoughts – and vice versa. Recall Descartes' insistence that the mind, the self, cannot be divided. Further, if Lefty shoots Righty dead, Lefty has not committed suicide.

Perhaps such an hypothesized neural operation as the above should count as the death of you; yet that sits uneasily with the thought that Lefty would be you, if Righty did not exist – and vice versa. To put it rhetorically, as does Derek Parfit who celebrated these scenarios, 'How could a double success be a failure?'

There are many variant replication tales, posing problems for understanding personal identity via psychological continuity. Arguably, the problems arise because we are wedded to 'identity'.

Maybe, especially when attending to duration, identity needs to be distinguished from remaining the same and surviving. We easily speak of the ship, tree, handbag being the same items as we saw last year, while recognizing that changes, even radical ones, have taken place: the ship has new sails, the tree is now in blossom, the handbag was recently patched.

Sameness through time, in contrast to identity, appears to permit matters of degree: the ship, tree and handbag are *to some degree* the same as before. If that is so, then perhaps we should become receptive to the thought that we – our consciousness – may divide: fission may occur. In our example, perhaps you are both to some degree Lefty and to some degree Righty, without thereby Lefty and Righty being identical – and arguably without, given the lack of direct causal connectedness between them, Lefty and Righty being to some degree the same item.

Consider the world as it is, without bizarre experiments in thought. You are to some degree the same as the teenager a few years ago and to a lesser degree the schoolchild many years previous. You, as you are now, will be to some degree the same as the person continuous with you twenty years on. That line of thinking, propounded by Ardon Lyon and noticed by very few, has gained recent prominence through Derek Parfit. Parfit turns away from personal identity. In revisionary mode, he tells us that what matters is survival, itself a matter of degree. Lyon sees that being the same, over time, is also a matter of degree.

If the interest that you hold for your forthcoming holiday and your pension in retirement is an interest in individuals who are only to some degree the same as you – in Parfit's terms, 'later selves' – then the apparent sharp contrast between self-interest and other-interest may weaken. Grasping your concern for your future as, in truth, being for future selves, to a greater or lesser degree similar to you, may generate the demand that, in all consistency, you should be concerned for other selves – other people – right now. Indeed, questions soon arise over the responsibilities we have now to provide for our later 'selves' and for others. Consider the fable:

> In summertime, the ant toils for his future winter self's benefit; the grasshopper just sings, prances and dances, living for the moment, for the sun. When the winters come, the ant has provisions, the grasshopper has none.

The question to ponder is: does the grasshopper in winter deserve his suffering because of his former self's reckless and feckless living? After all, he is not strictly identical with that former feckless self, according to Lyon and Parfit.

Securing consistency in treatment of individuals, if seeing those individuals as surviving only to some degree into the future, is far from easy. Further, there remains a seeming and vital distinction between those selves that are 'mine', possessing appropriate psychological chains or physical continuities, and those that are not. Further still, the whole enterprise of understanding my survival in terms of my memories, of my psychological continuity, may be vitiated by circularity. The psychological continuity requirement relies on, for example, my remembering *my* stealing the apples 'from within', not my remembering it solely as an historic event that Peter Cave stole the apples. Thus, care has to be taken over how the remembering is analysed in order to avoid circularity charges.

## Whether death is a harm

The focus on survival is likely to cause wonderment at survival's end, at death. We (maybe controversially) assume here that death is complete annihilation. Now, if we see our temporal continuation as a sequence of selves with varying degrees of similarity and connectedness, we are undergoing little deaths, so to speak, much of the time. You as an infant no longer exist; the later self, reading this book – to some degree continuous with that infant – will no longer exist next year. That later self will only have some continuity with the current self.

Some may embrace the above thought as comforting: survival is just a matter of various relations of similarity. Such relations can exist after the death of the body because others may be influenced by you, holding similar beliefs, attitudes and memories in some way connected with you.

By contrast, we who see our persistence as that of the continuing living biological entity know that that entity at some stage will cease to be. It is appropriate, then, to turn to a classic argument that, at heart, tells us not to worry about our mortality. It is pithily summed by the aphorism:

> When death is there, we are not; when we are there, death is not.

Thus spoke Epicurus. Epicurus, fourth century BC, was, of course, an Epicurean, but the understanding of 'Epicurean' has radically changed. Well-being, as promoted by Epicurus, does not involve desire for more and more sensuous pleasure. Well-being is perfect in the moment; it is not 'more perfect' by continuing for longer. Fear of death, according to Epicurus, leads to superstitions about afterlives or desperate obsessions to grab more in this life, thus corrupting everyday well-being. Lucretius, a Roman of the first century BC, produced explicit arguments designed to bolster Epicurus's position. Here comes one of the arguments:

Premiss 1: Events can be good or bad for individuals only if, at the time, the individuals are subjects of possible experiences.

Premiss 2: Deceased individuals are not subjects of possible experiences.

Conclusion 1:   Nothing can be good or bad for deceased
                individuals.
Premiss 3:      It is rational to fear things only if they will be
                bad for you.
Conclusion 2:   It is not rational to fear being a deceased
                individual.

The argument needs some tidying for it would show at best only
that events and states after death, not dying and death, cannot be
bad for – do not harm – the deceased. Tidying can occur easily
for the distinctive badness of dying is that it leads to death and
death to being dead.

The key trouble with the argument, we probably want to
say, is that individuals who die have lost all future. A quick
but mistaken retort is that, as those individuals did not have the
future years, how have they lost them? Such reasoning could
lead to the bad argument that we can never avoid accidents: after
all, the accidents have not happened and, if avoided, will not
happen.

Defending his position, Lucretius highlights the impossibility
of comparing those years of your post-death non-existence –
whatever value could be assigned to non-existence? – with
the extra living years, were you not to have died. The right
comparison, though, is that of an actual life-span with the possible longer life-span – and that latter has been lost. Further, the
person who died has probably lost something of value even
though he lacks existence and hence is unaware of that loss.
Bad things may happen to us – betrayal, for example, as seen
in Chapter One – even though we remain unaware of them.

Taking the above thought further, bad things may happen to
us, even though we no longer exist. Speaking metaphorically,
we extend beyond our skin, beyond our birth and death. We
may come to be harmed by events before our birth and, indi-
rectly, even before our conception – for example, through our

mother-to-be's drug abuse leaving her in a poor state of health. Indeed, we may see nature's unfairness in that some are born well and talented; others not. Luck egalitarians seek to compensate politically for life's unfairness, as we shall see in Chapter Five.

Arguably – and in opposition to Lucretius – the bad news is that we may also be harmed by events after our death, our annihilation, for example, through ruin of reputation, and not just through the severe limitation on the years that we, if truly biological entities, could exist within. Paradoxically, though, death may still be required to give meaning to life, to provide structure and substance to life, conditions necessary for engendering a good life, a flourishing life, a life with point – the topic for reflection in our Epilogue. The good life, though, also raises matters of morality; and so it is to morality that we turn – for how *ought* we to live?

# 4
# What – morally – ought we to do?

Your good friend Erskin rests on his death bed – more accurately, the bed soon to be such. Alone with him, you have just promised that, when he passes on, you too will pass on, will pass on his stash of cash to Laetitia, a young lady friend of his. She knows nothing about the money. Erskin duly dies and in your search for Laetitia, you discover that she is a rich courtesan, as Erskin well knew. You also find – to your amazement – that Erskin has daughters and a former wife, who speak fondly of him, clearly distressed by his death. They live in poverty. Indeed, you could do with some money yourself. What ought you to do?

One immediate thought is that it would be wrong for you to take the money for yourself, at least without further thought. It would be wrong, if we are considering what you ought *morally* to do. Morality and self-interest, at least on the surface, are distinct. Although sometimes they coincide – perhaps you morally ought to be the one saved from drowning – what we morally ought to do is not essentially a matter of pursuing our own wants and self-interest. That awareness raises the question of whether we can be motivated by moral duty alone or by the interests of others. We reflected, in Chapter Two, whether actions are always self-interested.

To return to Erskin, some would insist that you should never break a promise. Others would maintain it obvious that you should pass the money to the family, hence breaking your promise. Yet others may be more detached, arguing that the money ought to go to famine relief: 'Why be biased in favour of his family?' Your focus, in contrast, could be on your integrity, leading you to insist, 'I am not the sort of person who can break a promise.'

Those different answers manifest elements from distinct moral or ethical theories of considerable influence; so, to those we turn. Later, we shall wonder whether theoretical principles possess an essential role in our moral understanding; we shall, indeed, also note how a few philosophers use 'ethics' as a wider term than 'morality'.

To avoid confusion, it is worth remembering that key moral terms such as 'good', 'ought', 'right' and their opposites, have non-moral deployments. Maybe you ought to eat with a knife and fork, but that concerns custom and etiquette. If you go to war, you ought to have an exit strategy; if you seek power, you should be prepared to murder opponents. Such 'ought's and 'should's recommend means for achieving certain ends, without addressing the morality or immorality of the means or ends; they are amoral rather than necessarily immoral. Turning to the word 'good', we may speak of Myfanwy as being a good librettist, but that does not make her a good person. After all, good knives possess excellence in cutting – good thieves possess skills at thieving – but they thereby merit no moral accolades.

## Detachments: duties and consequences

Some people – most influentially, Immanuel Kant – insist that moral principles must hold fast: breaking a promise, for instance, is always morally wrong. In greater detail, there are moral principles that may be broken only if they clash with other higher moral principles. If the choice is between breaking a promise and murdering, then one principle has to give way to the other – and here it should be clear which way the choice goes – even though keeping promises and not murdering are both absolute duties.

The above is a deontological line, 'deon' meaning obligation. Moral duties are grounded in certain principles; those principles may be seen as determining individuals' basic rights. The line harmonizes with, though does not require, belief in divine commandments that demand human obedience. That belief is examined when, in Chapter Nine, we encounter God.

One immediate problem for deontologists is uncovering the moral principles. Some, as implied, turn to God. Kant, though, reasons his way to his much discussed 'categorical imperative', the grounding of all moral duties. That imperative comes in different formulations: we shall examine the central one later on. The underlying spirit is that we ought never to treat people *solely* as means to ends. We should respect human beings as autonomous – 'free', self-governing – agents with rights. Such respect requires, for example, that we always deal with people honestly, irrespective of consequences. Had we not kept our promise, we should have respected neither Erskin, an agent deserving the truth, nor our own rationality and dignity.

The Kantian deontological line clashes with another line, namely that there is but one overriding principle, one that rests all morality on consequences. The most influential 'consequentialist' doctrine is utilitarianism, typically associated with Jeremy Bentham and John Stuart Mill. Mr Bentham may still be seen, well, his auto icon – that is, his skeleton dressed in his clothes, surmounted by a waxen head – seated in University College London. According to utilitarianism, the right action is that with maximum utility, but 'utility' is not understood as usefulness; it is that which maximizes happiness or is likely to maximize happiness, though some utilitarians stress minimizing suffering. The theory is forward looking, turning to the future for determining what we morally should do now. The deontological stance, in contrast, is often backward looking: your duty now is determined by the past, for example, your earlier promises. Utilitarianism's classic formulation – Bentham's Greatest Happiness Principle – is that right actions are those that secure the greatest happiness of the greatest number. Of course, there are scholarly and practical debates about the nature of happiness and how to determine likely consequences. In the Erskin scenario, it may be known that the cash would generate negligible additional happiness for Laetitia, but would be of considerable benefit to others. The benefit may be even greater to the former wife and daughters, if you added the little falsehood that Erskin wanted them to inherit. Arguably, Erskin, now deceased, suffers not at all from the broken promise. So, on utilitarian grounds, you ought to break your promise, ignoring Chapter Three's argument that posthumous harms can exist, and give the money to the needy family – unless greater overall benefit would likely be achieved, were the money spread more widely, for example, distributed through charities for famine victims.

Suppose Erskin's daughters do receive some of the money; as a result they fall into buying drugs, ruining their lives, perhaps becoming pregnant, giving birth to offspring who develop into mass murderers – or discoverers of malaria cures, saving millions of lives. Such consequences are possible, but we have no good reason to expect them. Utilitarians – as do we all – have to rely on reasonable assumptions. On the surface, the utilitarian sea is unruffled by moral anguishes: it presents a simple principle for assessing right actions.

Below utilitarianism's smooth surface are ripples of problematic distribution. Yes, everyone's happiness counts in calculating the right action; but possibly happiness maximization would occur if some people were slaves, their misery outweighed by the rest of society's happiness. Utilitarianism, its critics insist, values people merely as containers for happiness. In line with that thought, perhaps one way of maximizing happiness is to create more and more people each with a small overall happiness; yet we may feel that a better world would be one with less happiness overall (as fewer people), yet each person considerably happier. After all, we are not (are we?) depriving non-existent people of anything by not creating them. Pithily put, should we maximize happiness by making more happy people or making people more happy?

Happiness is often understood as pleasure and absence of pain. Bentham quietly wrote in teeny handwriting that, if the same quantity of pleasure results, then pushpin is as good as poetry, pushpin being a child's game. Mind you, some scurrilously suggest that 'pushpin' is a euphemism for sexual intercourse. Mill, much influenced by Bentham, for and against, and who read his teeny writing, challenged the pushpin-poetry equivalence, arguing that some pleasures are 'higher', are more valuable, than others. Utilitarianism is often understood as simply promoting the satisfaction of desires, but that certainly is not Mill's utilitarianism: the desires may be for the lower pleasures of pushpin, football and sex – in contrast to the higher pleasures of poetry, philosophy and friendship. Mill famously claimed: 'tis better to be a dissatisfied Socrates than a satisfied pig. With the swine to the fore, we should note that Mill does recognize – as does Bentham – that in assessing overall happiness the sufferings of animals are included. Bentham wrote that the moral question concerning individuals is neither can they reason nor can they talk, but simply can they suffer? Bentham hoped for a time 'when humanity will extend its mantle over everything which breathes'. Bentham is an early anti-speciesist: we should not ignore the suffering of members of another species just because they are of another species.

Mill's preference for the Socratic over the swinish is no aberrant idiosyncrasy: we readily recognize some lives as more fulfilled than others – and Mill's stress is on happiness in the wide sense of 'flourishing'. Flourishing involves achievements and engagements with the world. Recalling Chapter One's experience machine, we may speculate that Mill would not recommend such plugging, though he would probably value people's freedom to make such experiential choices.

Mill's utilitarianism led – maybe surprisingly so – to his highly influential Liberty Principle. Mill promotes liberty: in order to have the chance to flourish, people require opportunities – the so-called negative liberty – enabling them to seek to realize themselves as autonomous, self-governing agents, possessing the so-called positive liberty. There are obvious problems with self-realization as a moral good: we are not keen on the self-realization of the expert thief or fraudster. Hence, Mill's Liberty Principle enjoins maximum liberty consistent with not harming others.

The Liberty Principle clashes, it has been argued, with Mill's utilitarianism: perhaps happiness would be maximized if people were encouraged to conform. Perhaps happiness would be maximized if choices were restricted: think how we may dither between so many consumer goods; think how we can foolishly succumb to immediate desires. A response in Mill's spirit, to the implied preference for paternalism, of telling people how to run their lives, is that happiness requires autonomy; autonomy is an essential component of flourishing.

Understanding Mill's happiness in terms of a multifaceted flourishing – with higher and lower pleasures, with values of autonomy, friendship, even nobility and dignity – is at odds with the attractions (for some) of unreformed utilitarianism, namely the homogeneity or simplicity of the happiness value for calculations. Once we recognize the different values in a flourishing life, we see that there is no common currency – of pleasures, of hedonist units – into which they can all be cashed and hence measured. Hence, it can be mysterious how we do manage to 'weigh up' different considerations in order to decide what to do.

## Attachments

Although utilitarians and deontologists deploy different reasoning, often providing different answers to Erskin-type dilemmas, they possess a key similarity: they take a detached view of the situation and apply moral principles or the single consequentialist principle. Utilitarians step back and judge likely overall happiness, taking into account one and all: they seek to be neutral, detached, impartial. Their own interests count, but hold no privileged position. Deontologists reason to principles that hold good for all, impartially. A criticism of both is that they are too detached, too impartial, to capture morality's wide-ranging concerns.

Focusing on the individual agent can lead to the above criticism. What do you need to be happy, to flourish? The starting point, the criticism goes, should be oneself, one's own happiness – egoism and hedonism. That appears in conflict with morality's essential 'other' concern; yet morality may still be brought into play, even from such a starting position.

The starting position, typically associated with Aristotle, is that human beings seek happiness, prosperity, flourishing. Those three terms translate the Greek *eudaimonia*. Now, Mill's utilitarianism aims at maximum flourishing overall; but Aristotelianism – these days revised as 'virtue theory' – focuses on the kind of human beings we should seek to be, given our aim for personal flourishing. There are, it is argued, some basic character traits that promote flourishing, while allowing that people secure fulfilment in different ways. No character set guarantees a flourishing life, but certain traits increase likelihoods. Here is a typical analogy: it is prudent not to smoke, even though non-smoking does not guarantee freedom from lung cancer and smoking does not always lead to lung cancer. Well, which traits are most likely to lead to human flourishing…? By the way, we have not forgotten your promise to Erskin; we shall return in due course.

Consider your children – or brothers or sisters. Would you want them to grow up as liars and cheats, mean and unfair? No doubt deceit may sometimes be necessary; but overall you probably prefer other people and yourself to be truthful, fair and kind. Consider politicians who climb the greasy pole by deception, back-stabbing and ruthlessness. Contrast with politicians who achieve success without such dealings (true, we optimistically assume that is possible). The former would not be trusted, would be slated behind their backs; the latter would have true friends and feel comfortable with themselves. Maybe presidents and prime ministers need occasionally to dirty their hands, as Machiavelli would argue, engaging in deceptions, even assassinations, for the nation's protection; but generally people prefer success achieved in the right way – through being fair, honest and trustworthy, through generosity and, of course, being wisely tuned to the facts. Such character traits are deemed 'virtues' because their cultivation typically promotes a flourishing life.

Now, if you maintain friendships and show kindness out of pure self-interest – to have people 'owing you' in case you fall into need – then you would probably not feel that good about yourself. If others discovered your motivation, they would feel used, the friendship tainted; they probably would not stay around for long. Hence, true friendship and kindness require that you are interested in others for their sake. Possession of the virtues requires possessing the right motivations. Thus it is that virtue theory pulls away from the egoistic hedonism charge.

And so, we return to Erskin. In terms of modern virtue theory, what would a wise and virtuous person do? Well, it is difficult to know, if you are not already wise and virtuous – and if not wise and virtuous, it may be difficult to spot someone who is. However wise and virtuous someone may be though, it is far from obvious that a definitive right answer would surface for Erskin; but that may be an advantage – for many (though not all) moral decisions are genuine dilemmas, depending in part on what the individual concerned could proudly live with and defend. The wise and virtuous person should be compassionate and may therefore be moved by the distress of Erskin's family – and hence be prepared to break the promise. Yet we could imagine an unbending man of integrity, firm to his promise-keeping – and proud of it.

There are cases and cases, ways of looking, without a right answer applicable to all. Arguably, that is an important feature of morality, a feature to which neither deontology nor utilitarianism gives adequate voice.

## THREE APPROACHES TO MORALITY

# Where to look

*Utilitarianism*: into the future, at the consequences or likely consequences of actions.

*Deontology*: at rights, at the treatment individuals should rightly expect from others.

*Virtue Theory*: at one's character, the sort of person to be.

# What to look for

*Utilitarianism*: how to maximize happiness overall.

*Deontology*: duties that we could all rationally accept as universal, without contradiction.

*Virtue theory*: character traits that are likely to promote a flourishing life for us.

# Key advantages

*Utilitarianism*: unprejudiced concern for overall welfare, avoidance of suffering, including that of non-human animals.

*Deontology*: manifestation of universal respect for individual people and their autonomy.

*Virtue theory*: recognition that morality involves particular attachments and dilemmas.

# Key disadvantages

*Utilitarianism*: its detached stance threatens to sacrifice particular individuals for the general welfare; it thus needs supplements for a fair distribution of happiness.

*Deontology*: leaves it unclear how rights are discovered, which take priority; it appears inflexible and cold.

*Virtue theory*: gives rise to the danger of morality as culturally relative, with no clear rules to follow.

## More on the theories

Deontology and utilitarianism seek detached perspectives, but the Aristotelian approach guides us towards the agent's perspective, the agent enmeshed in the world: an attached or agent-centred view. For example, we may place loyalty to family over total fairness; we may value close attachments over those less intimate. Using E. M. Forster's example, we may prefer to betray our country rather than our friends. The mother naturally saves her son rather than the unknown child. Such examples tell us not merely what we may do or what comes naturally, but sometimes what we ought to do. Could we live a life totally detached, totally impartial? What would it be like? Consider a recent complaint, namely that of speciesism, mentioned earlier.

Speciesism is said to be akin to sexism and racism. It manifests discrimination against other species without good reason: chimps are experimented on, but not babies. Pigs are eaten for food, but not humans. Now, the suffering of non-human animals merits moral concern, but, if able to save only one creature, it does not mean that rescuing the pet cat rather than the child should be a serious consideration. Of course, that some things come naturally to us does not remotely show that they are therefore the right things to do. Many natural inclinations – maybe those of greed, revenge, hate – should typically be overcome. We rightly recognize, though, some partialities as morally important and others not; but there is no magical prior rule, plucked from the heavens, telling us how to do this.

♈

Utilitarianism, as implied, can make a big gesture in the Aristotelian direction by understanding happiness as flourishing. Although it is a detached theory – everyone's happiness to be counted – it can recognize that flourishing requires certain partialities.

Further, the utilitarian aim should not be seen as giving us our day-by-day motivations. As John Austin, a one-time utilitarian friend of Mill, wrote, the utilitarian does not consult the common welfare before kissing his mistress; such calculations would radically undermine loving relationships and hence happiness. Suppose two people needing a kidney transplant, one your close friend, the other someone not of your acquaintance – and you are prepared to donate a kidney. To think about which person to aid would be 'one thought too many'. Even if the thinking led you to conclude in favour of your friend – you calculate that encouragement of friendships helps in maximizing happiness – you would have shown yourself to lack friendship's spontaneity. Just to think about what we ought to do, instead of acting on right feelings, sometimes displays undesirable or corrupt characters.

Utilitarianism may also gesture towards some deontological principles, principles not directly justified by consequences. After all, maximum happiness may best be secured if most people do *not* believe in utilitarianism, but accept fixed principles, develop stable dispositions to be fair, never to kill and so forth. Thus it is that we may now see how utilitarians, of a certain ilk, could encourage you to be so disposed that even in the Erskin case, you would not break your promise, despite promise-breaking on that occasion leading to greater overall happiness than promise-keeping.

The above reasoning manifests one line of indirect utilitarianism: it contrasts with the reasoning of basic direct (or act) utilitarianism, first presented, where the right action is discovered by applying utilitarian calculations to each action between which choices have to be made. Indirect utilitarianism can be seen as 'government house': we moral philosophers, 'colonial rulers' so to speak, know that the ultimate aim is greatest happiness, but to achieve it, people must follow some simple moral rules and not perform their own calculations.

There is another indirect version, rule utilitarianism: it identifies the right action as that which maximizes happiness if everyone performed that type of action. Were everyone to break promises whenever it suited them, as opposed always to keeping promises, then, if known, happiness would not be maximized for no one could be trusted. Rule utilitarianism, though, collapses into act utilitarianism, if the contending rules are allowed complexity. After all, maybe the best rule, were it to be universally followed is: never break promises except when, by so doing, promise-keeping is not undermined and happiness is maximized. On such a basis, breaking the promise to Erskin would again be justified – for no one, other than you, need know about the broken promise.

$$\gamma$$

'What if everyone were to do likewise' has moral impact for many: but should it, if you know that everyone will not do likewise? Were everyone to boycott factory-farmed meat, then supermarket buying practices would change: factory farming and hence animal suffering would be reduced, arguably outweighing the resultant distress for meat-loving humans. If so, rule utilitarians should advocate such boycotts – and so you ought to resist buying the meat. Act utilitarian reasoning, in contrast, focuses on your individual acts of meat purchase. The animal – the meat – is already dead; your purchase or non-purchase will go unnoticed by the supermarket and – dare I add – you are no major celebrity who sets trends that others follow. Paradoxical matters arise. Consider the following.

In the vast majority of cases your particular vote makes no relevant difference to the outcome of a national election. Therefore, do not bother to vote (unless it makes you especially happy); instead do something with greater happiness potential – the ironing, gardening or visiting depressed parents. Yet were everyone to follow non-voting recommendations, electoral

processes would collapse. Rest assured, though: not everyone
will follow the recommendation. Indeed, Henry Sidgwick, an
important nineteenth-century utilitarian, espousing 'government
house' utilitarianism, recommended keeping the utilitarian basis
of morality hidden from the mass of people. The recommendation occurs in his long dusty volume of ethics; so he could be
confident that most people would not read of the proposed
deception.

Utilitarians, of whatever flavour, suffer the basic criticism that
they are interested in individuals merely as happiness containers.
If killing one healthy person releases his organs for transplant,
thus saving the lives of others – transplanted heart for Heather,
liver for Laurence, kidneys for Kate and Kiki and so forth – then
that is what morally ought to be done, unless knowledge of the
policy seeps out, causing healthy people the misery of 'we could
be next'. As already mentioned, if maximum happiness would be
secured by having slaves whose misery is outweighed by the
overall happiness of others, then slavery it is. Utilitarianism, unless
modified, lacks respect for human beings. Even if – because of
distress resulting from insecurity – utilitarianism rejects the killing of innocent people for others' benefit, many would feel that
that was not the right reason against killing.

Human beings, it is often insisted, possess rights: a right to life,
a right to their organs. Such 'human rights' talk is murky, especially when declarations of human rights risk placing the rights
to life and freedom of speech in the same list as rights to holidays
and maternity leave. Arguably 'rights' talk, outside the legal
context, simply draws attention to highly regarded universal
principles – trump cards to be played. It is just wrong to kill an
innocent person – full stop. And that, skipping pass the full stop,
returns us to Kant who, as intimated, stressed respect for people
as moral agents. Let us view a little Kant.

Morality requires that we perceive ourselves as autonomous
agents who can choose to do what we ought to do: 'ought'

implies 'can' as introduced in Chapter Two. We are not free autonomous agents when rocked by desires, passions and emotions; they come unbidden. Now, hypothetical imperatives announce what ought to be done, *if*... If you want to visit the club, then you ought to wear trousers. If you desire wealth, become a lawyer. To avoid dependence on such unbidden desires, we need to consider categorical imperatives, imperatives that lack 'iffy' conditions based on biological contingencies. That suggests to Kant that morality must be universal and reason-based, just as, always and everywhere, $2 + 2 = 4$, even on Pluto, whatever your desires or Plutonian desires. Kant offers a universalizing test, the Formula of Universal Law, for deriving particular imperatives:

Act only on that maxim through which you can at the same time will that it should become a universal law.

That sounds like utilitarianism with its 'rule' modification, but utilitarian reasoning concerns maximizing happiness; Kant focuses on logical consistency. A contradiction arises, he claims, if we will that people break promises whenever it suits them – for then no promises would ever be accepted, thus undermining, 'contradicting', the promise-keeping institution. Were we to will that people commit suicide whenever they wanted, that too would 'contradict' nature – well, so Kant announces, though it is difficult to see how.

Kant's reasoning deserves challenge at every step. Consider the universalizing test: 'universalizability'. We cannot consistently will – can we? – the universal law that everyone is a net seller of women's hats for there would then be no net buyers; yet surely the trade of milliner is not morally disreputable. Furthermore, by grounding morality in reason, Kant is led to insist that moral deeds must be motivated by a sense of duty. Woe is she who helps the beggar because moved by compassion: she fails to act from duty; she merits no moral gold stars. Virtue theory stands in sharp contrast – people should be driven by virtues such as compassion – and utilitarians would argue that being compassionately disposed may well promote overall happiness.

Why does Kant reject feelings as key to *moral* motivations? Well, he seeks to separate morality from luck, a separation already encountered concerning responsibility. We cannot help our biological characteristics, whether we are born compassionate or cold, generous or mean; but reason's moral dictates are accessible to us as rational agents. That, of course, also deserves challenge: just as some people possess greedy natures, so some lack grasp of moral duties.

Kantian deontological theories – and utilitarian theories – are deployed to deliver definitive answers about what morally ought to be done. That deployment closes eyes to the tragedy within which we may find ourselves – where, whatever we do, which-ever way we jump, we have done something wrong as well as, perhaps, something right. The rightness does not cancel the wrongness; and the wrongdoing may generate regrets – remorse and shame – despite its being the right thing to do.

## Dilemmas, conflicts and cases

Morality embraces a motley mash of concerns: saving lives, welfare, justice, compassion, courage, freedom, loyalty, forgive-ness, remorse – and so forth. So, it is unsurprising that the three theories above each give voice to genuine moral features, yet each suffers deficiencies as seen. Even when addressing a single value, we meet conflict: loyalty to Maria may require disloyalty to Martina. Conflicts all the more readily arise when different values are in play: you must break a promise to Ben in order to help Den. Conflicts may, indeed, take our values beyond morality: perhaps moral values should not be overriding. Even if morality dictates that you ought not to sacrifice your son, maybe the sacrifice is your religious duty and takes priority – as told in the Torah's tale of Abraham being tested by Yahweh. Even if morality tells you that you must not abandon your parents, your artistic impulse may dictate otherwise: the life of the creative poet or the Antarctic explorer may have its own intrinsic value, one that trumps the life of moral duty. The term 'ethics', now distinguished from 'morality', can be deployed to highlight important values, ones that stretch beyond moral duty, ones that mark a wider ethos, challenging morality as of overiding importance.

Placing the wider concerns of ethics aside, a moral *theory* determines, in many cases at least, what people ought to do or, at least, what they ought not to do. A moral theory needs to harmonize with those basic beliefs, attitudes and practices that many people recognize as right or good. It displays certain underlying principles which, when consistently applied, may assist us in deciding the right action in difficult cases. The utilitarian concern for avoidance of suffering may, for example, encourage people to extend the moral embrace beyond humans to other animals. Confidence in the power of theory, though, should not be great. Here is why.

A moral theory, for example Kant's deontology, includes as a derived principle that it is wrong to kill innocent human life. Supplement that thought with the observation that allowing people to die generates the same outcome as killing. Reflection on that may lead us to treat our failure to aid people dying from famine as more or less morally equivalent to killings from afar. Yet our moral sense – our emotional convenience? – rebels against such a conclusion. In not giving to famine relief we surely are not as bad as mass murderers. The result may be that we now build into our moral theory a justification for distinguishing between killing and letting die. We move from individual cases in the first place to theory, yet modify the theory when seeing how it applies to other individual cases and our moral intuitions.

The three moral approaches discussed each need revision, once tested against our seemingly clear moral convictions regarding particular cases. In undiluted crude forms, utilitarianism has scant regard for rights and partialities, whereas deontology, certainly Kant's original, too rigidly sticks to principles, while virtue theory arguably is excessively wishy-washy. Those thoughts may tempt us into an eclectic theory that cherry picks. An alternative is to challenge the value of theory. Important moral considerations vary from context to context. Lying about 'final' offers in wage negotiations is different from lying in the House of Lords. Further, theories, as implied, are not ultimately derived from abstract heavens, but are grounded in our intuitions about particular cases. True, the Kantian 'never lie' principle may initially tempt, but when faced with the mad axe-man, seeking our neighbours to axe, most people – in contrast to Kant – conclude that lying can be right, the lie resulting in the axe-man landing in the arms of the police. Such considerations can lead to 'particularism' in morality, an approach drawing away from principles, both in theory and practice.

Particularism's stress on deciding moral matters, case by case, does not show that 'anything goes' or that 'anything ought to go'. It does not show that morality is culturally relative or merely a matter of how a subject feels. If the particular action is torturing innocent bystanders for sheer fun, then that action may be recognized as morally wrong full stop. There are, though, arguments about the meaning of moral terms and the nature of moral properties – an area of philosophy known as 'meta-ethics' – that tempts some away from the assumed moral objectivity implied throughout the above discussion. So, time to turn briefly to some meta-ethical lines and whether morality may be no more than, for example, a boo and hurrah.

## THE RIGHT TO LIFE: A THOUGHT EXPERIMENT

You are in hospital for a minor procedure, but when you awake, you find a man seated beside you. Tubing runs between you and him, plugging him into your blood supply. Doctors explain. The man had been rushed into casualty, nearing death. He needed special lymphocytes which only your blood can supply. So long as he remains plugged into you, he is fine and so are you. Well, so are you – except for the inconvenience. Wherever you go, he goes too.

# Moral concerns

The man has a right to life, but does he have a right to use of your body? Do you have a right to unplug him – although it will lead to his death? Even if he lacks the right to use of your body, would it be morally impermissible to unplug him?

# The Minimally Decent Samaritan

Many rights rest on contracts. The right to life involves no contract: perhaps it is a 'natural right', in virtue of being human. Even if so, that surely does not allow people a right to use of your body without consent. Their right to life is not the right to whatever is required for life – such as your blood, organs, money and home.

Arguably, you have the right to unplug him – as trespasser – yet it may still be wrong to do so: it would be unkind. The example, from Judith Jarvis Thomson, introduces the Minimally Decent Samaritan who recognizes that morality extends beyond 'rights' into the virtues – compassion, generosity, courage. Yet how long would it be minimally decent to assist the intruder before 'enough is enough'? When is the moral burden too heavy?

# Abortion

The original tale had abortion in focus. *Even if* the foetus is a person, its right to life does not mean a right to be carried. Even if women have rights over their bodies, it can still be wrong to exercise those rights. In cases of pregnancy – and of the plugged-in man – what it is minimally decent to do is not just a matter of rights.

# Yelps

Realists argue that moral properties are worldly features – out there, independently of us – just as are the weight, size and colours of physical objects. Mention of colour, though, should alert us to questions about 'out there'. Our visual sensations of reds and greens are caused by external objects impinging on optic nerves, but the objects 'in themselves' do not thereby resemble those colourful sensations. Non-realists may take their cue from colour: moral properties, correctly understood, are just features of human beings resulting from certain interactions. They are not *objective*, that is, existing independently of how we feel. Let us see how this works.

When the goal was scored, Zeki yelped hurrahs, whereas Sophie just groaned, but when the opera came to town, Sophie smiled with pleasure; it was Zeki's groaning time. Neither made explicit statements *that* such and such is so and so; their yelps, shouts and groans simply expressed different attitudes – approval, disapproval – to the events. With no statements made, no scope for formal contradiction arose. True, behind those yelps were implicit statements, but the statements went on different tracks. Zeki would have stated that he felt pangs of approval for the goals; Sophie's statements would have been that she disapproved. And so it may be with seeming judgements of morality. 'You ought not to have killed that man' is akin to a loud boo at that killing. More accurately, the analysis is dualistic, with the descriptive 'You killed him' combined with the emotional and expressive 'boo'.

When Kramer says that liver is nice and George says not, they come to no blows. They recognize that there exist no worldly features of nice and nasty, independent of particular fancies. They are expressing their subjective tastes. In similar fashion, on the moral 'emotivism' just outlined, there are no moral facts 'out there', but only individuals expressing or maybe stating their likes and dislikes – and perhaps, in contrast to mere tastes, also eager to persuade listeners to follow in attitudinal train. So-called moral statements are at heart expressions of emotion and arguably exhortations, encouraging people to act accordingly. A source for this line of thinking is David Hume with his stress on our sentiments as key to moral judgements.

The temptation towards emotivism and similar non-cognitivist theories – non-cognitivism in that there are no worldly moral facts to cognize, to get to know – is the following. Were there moral facts independent of human beings, they would be most peculiar, queer, nothing like facts investigated by scientists. Alleged moral *facts* tell us how we *ought* to behave – they are prescriptive – and hence differ radically from the descriptive. It is one thing to say, for example, that it is a fact that philosophizing will maximize happiness, but something very different to say that it is a fact that people *ought* to maximize happiness.

The argument from queerness, just sketched, is associated with the so-called error theory of morality. The theory accepts, contrasting with emotivism, that moral statements are statements, indeed statements about the world: it is just that they are false statements. The world does not contain moral facts.

Arguably, emotivism and error theory both rely on blinkered views of what objective facts can be. After all, the truths of mathematics are radically different from truths about the physical world, yet we do not cast mathematics into the seas of emotivism, error or subjectivisms. Although we recognize that our sensations of colours depend in part on the biological, we do not conclude that there is no objective difference between red balloons and yellow balloons that grounds the colour distinction.

♈

Wittgenstein wrote of how, in philosophy, there is a (mistaken) craving for generality. We have seen that craving in philosophers' eagerness to construct moral theories. So too, we may see that craving in some philosophers' determination to reject moral facts or truths as being truly facts or truths, as if all facts or truths must be analysable by scientific investigation.

In fact – and in truth – many of our descriptions carry valuations within. It is a fact that Petronella made a promise – and that can tell us what she ought to do next. It may be a fact that Barendina is benevolent, Michelle magnanimous, and Nicole noble – and hence they are rightly to be commended. Many things that we say about the world have intertwined within both descriptive and evaluative elements – and it is perhaps a mistake to think that those elements can be separated. Such separation may be as doubtful as the dualism of Chapter One that endeavours to understand all human actions in terms of a psychological component – an intention, for example – and a bodily behavioural component. To sum up the moral here, let us deploy and modify a Shakespearean quotation, one used by Wittgenstein:

Philosophy needs to teach us differences.

# 5

# Political philosophy: what justifies the state?

Suppose an individual, Original, finds herself on a deserted desert island – a female Robinson Crusoe. She can get by: perhaps she knows how to build a shelter, catch selected fish and make fires for cooking. If we like, let us suppose additionally that she has landed with solar panels, bedroom equipment, even a traditional record player with eight preferred discs of music. She is content. All is well with her until…

All is well until one day another person, she discovers, lurks on the island, an island all but deserted except for two. The individual intrudes upon Original's life; he takes some of Original's equipment for his own use as well as some of the fish she has recently caught, some fruit she was ripening. 'But these are mine,' insists Original. 'Now, if you ask nicely I may share my fish, even, so to speak, my bed; but you have no right to take my possessions without consent. They are mine – and that should be enough to prohibit your grabbing.'

Intruder replies that Original has no right to those items – and furthermore, without her help he will be unable to survive. If, astonishingly, we graft onto our scenario a god with appropriate godly powers, should that god intervene to protect Original's property or, instead, should he side with Intruder, taking some of Original's property for Intruder's benefit? And how far should the god go? Should he provide Intruder with just sufficient for life – or sufficient for a leisurely life? Should equality of goods between Original and Intruder be the best outcome?

♈

Our small scenario gives rise to concerns within political philosophy. What (if anything) rightfully belongs to someone, what justifies 'this is mine' – when said of a variety of items, from those essential to life and health to the mishmash valued by some: champagne, cars, catamarans – even philosophy classes? 'Mine', noted Rousseau, is a frequent source of strife. A related question is: what gives authority to some – the state, the law – to rule over people, determining what is justly mine, what we may do and keep? We are compelled to wear clothes in public on the hottest of days, maybe fight for country, king or dictator, and pay taxes for health, education and welfare provision – for governmental limousines and funding for arts, sports, even royal celebrations.

Returning to Original on the desert island, in quick summary, would she be violated if some power compels her to transfer some of her goods to Intruder? Would the answer partially depend on Intruder's characteristics – how desperate he is; whether his plight results from laziness or bad luck? Would the answer partially depend on characteristics of Original – how she acquired her goods, whether she had consented to authorities deciding such matters? It is to that very last consideration that we first turn.

# The state of nature – and consent

Seeming violations of people are not usually treated as violations if the people concerned consent. Hence, one approach – a voluntarist approach – justifies a state's actions when and only when the individuals have consented to the state's power. Voluntarism, though, immediately requires qualification. If citizens are set to harm others, then we may claim that anyone – the state and individuals – ought to intrude without the would-be perpetrator's consent. If Flora is about to kill an unwilling Miles, we are right to intervene against Flora. Even that qualification to the crude voluntarist claim itself needs qualification. Some immoralities may be recognized as immoralities, yet of no governmental concern. Perhaps breaking promises is morally wrong, yet a wrong which, people standardly feel, justifies no state intrusion when in private life.

Do we consent to the laws of the land? Most of us usually obey the law, but largely by default or through fear of punishment. If we choose to evade paying tax, for example, we may be fined or imprisoned. In terms of Chapter Two, our negative liberty is restricted: opportunities are available, but at a cost – and the cost may be so great that we lack an effective liberty.

From Plato onwards, political philosophers have mused upon a state of nature – the state when human beings existed prior to government. Some philosophers apparently believed that they could describe such an actual state; of course, they could not – and we may challenge its relevance, if they could. Describing how things come about – the *genesis* – may be no guide to how things ought now to be. To think otherwise manifests a genetic fallacy, one that is sometimes made by scientists bedazzled by evolution theory. Evolutionary explanations of why we have greater concern for our families than for those far away do not in themselves demonstrate that is how things ought to be.

Let us see how the state of nature may be hypothesized and made relevant.

Thomas Hobbes – a pessimist (or maybe realist) about human nature in its 'natural' state – understood the state of nature as one of war, that is, one in which individuals would minimally have always to be on guard against others. That is so, argued Hobbes, because human beings, or at least some, naturally seek eminence – to have more possessions, superior power, or greater sexual success than others. Even ignoring the desire for eminence, there would be times when resources for all to live well, or just get by, would be inadequate; so, some individuals would lose out to the stronger, be the strength by way of brute force, guile or intelligence. The strong, though, could not rest complacent in their strength: even strong individuals need sleep and, when sleeping, the weak could temporarily gang up and kill.

Hobbes's view of human nature, he maintained, is supported by observation, of how people typically lack mutual trust, locking up their goods – and traditionally, we may add, some men even their wives. Others respond that such evidence is of human nature corrupted by competitive – now capitalist – structures: without those structures, people would be naturally cooperative. That optimistic line could possibly be the truth; but, given as we are now, we still need to assess what justifies the state's authority. Further, even if the state of nature initially is relatively benign, as John Locke (writing soon after Hobbes) insisted, a few people would, no doubt, lapse into killing others, into rape and pillage – and considerable conflicts would doubtless arise, when resources grew scarce. In summary, if, on the one hand, the state of nature is benign, with only cooperative individuals, it would be irrational to move to a full-blown state, with powers of coercion. If, on the other hand, the state of nature is nasty, lacking all cooperation, then it would seem irrational to risk agreeing with others to accept an overseeing authority; why believe others could be trusted? Indeed, there is some inconsistency regarding that 'other hand' for reaching agreements implies language, and language presupposes considerable pre-existing cooperation.

♈

## THREE INFLUENTIAL POLITICAL PHILOSOPHERS

**Thomas Hobbes** (1588–1679) – an atheist in religion, absolutist in politics, yet a great survivor (he lived to 91) – suffered years of civil war. In his *Leviathan*, he argued for an absolute sovereign to keep people in awe, without which, in a state of nature, a state of war, every man is on guard against every man and...

> there is no place for industry, because the fruit thereof is uncertain: and consequently no culture of the earth; no navigation, nor use of the commodities that may be imported by sea; no commodious building... no knowledge of the face of the earth; no account of time; no arts; no letters; no society; and which is worst of all, continual fear, and danger of violent death.

In those circumstances, Hobbes continues, life is solitary, poor, nasty, brutish and short. We add: Thomas, things could be worse: such a life could be solitary, poor, nasty, brutish and long.

**John Locke** (1632–1704) spent time as an Oxford don, a horticulturist and much else including being implicated in an attempted regicide. Locke, as did the poet John Milton earlier, emphasized consent and toleration through a social contract giving people the right to overthrow corrupt rulers. Arguably, Locke's work provided a blueprint for the American Constitution.

**Jean-Jacques Rousseau** (1712–1778) has been viewed as a great democrat and liberal, observing:

> Man was born free; and everywhere he is in chains. One thinks himself the master of others, and still remains a greater slave than they. How did this change come about? I do not know. What can make it legitimate? That question I think I can answer.

Rousseau's answer is for people to make a social contract, themselves mysteriously constituting the sovereign – with a general will that determines the interests of all. Woe betide you, if you disagree with that will: you are then forced to be free. Rousseau's liberal credentials can collapse into totalitarianism with the state's total control over its citizens' lives – in their true best interests, of course...

Instead of speculating what a state of nature would actually have been like, we may treat it as a theoretical construction for a thought-experiment. Pre-government – and with the pretence that individuals are rational – what would be agreed regarding laws necessary for a desirable society? Suppose it is rational for the pretended individuals to agree upon a common authority. Suppose too the existence of common interests, so a social contract can be reached such that they entrust their lives and liberty to an authority which acts in their interests. Supposing all that, do we have a voluntarist justification for obeying the authorities who rule over us now? Well, certainly not obviously so.

First, the current authorities may lack the characteristics rationally agreed upon under the above suppositions. Secondly, even with such characteristics, how does that supposed agreement establish that we *now* voluntarily consent? None of us is so old as to have lived in any past state of nature and few of us give explicit consent to the current state. The response is that we may manifest *tacit* consent. By staying within this society, walking the King's Highway (as Locke expressed it), maybe taking part in elections, we are tacitly agreeing to the state's authority.

The 'tacit' defence can quickly be knocked down – and David Hume skilfully knocked. Hume tells of a man on a ship in the raging ocean: does his on-board presence manifest tacit consent to the captain's orders? Obviously not: whether staying on board exhibits consent partially depends on alternatives available – in this case, the alternative is that of drowning in frightening seas. In order to emigrate, we need passports, money, a preparedness to leave friends and employment; we also need an acceptable country ready to receive us. Were, indeed, our presence under a government sufficient to show consent – and were consent sufficient to justify a government's rightful authority – then all manner of dictatorships and regimes would be properly authorized. That is a highly undesirable conclusion, not least for those who seek to justify government by means of a social contract: only certain types of government are meant to be justified, namely those that act in the common interests.

Arguably, voluntarism is the wrong target for securing the state's justification; perhaps the justification is simply that we reap benefits. Socrates, when refusing to escape a death sentence lawfully imposed by the Athenians, partially justified his refusal because of benefits earlier received from the state; further, it would be ungracious and unjust to reject the state's laws when it suited him. Many of us, of course, do receive significant benefits from society: our lives go better because of the stability imposed by the law, because of the services and protections provided.

Even if 'benefits received' is morally weighty, it fails to justify the state to those overall disadvantaged and to those who would reap greater benefits under different authorities. That is, the 'benefits received' justification is without universal application. Further, 'benefits received' arguably lacks moral weight: why should benefits unsought place us under resultant duties? If people buy you unrequested drinks, it is far from obvious that they deserve return favours – even if you lap up the drinks. Maybe you ought not to accept the drinks, but many state services are difficult to refuse. Street lighting exists outside your home; you cannot easily decline that benefit – except perhaps by blindfolding yourself.

Let us try the voluntarist justification of the state afresh. To what would we have consented, had we been rational and in the 'original position' of a state of nature with all its turmoil and uncertainties? We may well have traded certain freedoms for safety and other potential benefits. Is not that justification enough for obedience to a state providing such benefits? The answer is often 'no'. The approach typically receives the sharp dismissal that a hypothetical contract is not worth the paper it is not written upon. A hypothetical win on the lottery is no lottery win. Clearly hypothetical consent is not actual consent, but, contrary to the brusque dismissal, hypothetical consents can possess equivalent moral force to the actual.

Suppose a woman, hit by a reckless rickshaw, is seriously injured, but still conscious. People ask if she wants an ambulance called; she readily consents. Suppose a similar scenario, save that the woman is knocked unconscious. It is reasonable to call the ambulance on the basis of the hypothetical: it is what she would have consented to, had she been conscious. True, that is not actual consent; but it is akin in value. Of course, hypothetical consent possesses the *epistemic* problem – a knowledge problem – of what would indeed have received consent; but, even with explicit consent, we may have similar problems, for example, of knowing whether it has been properly informed.

## Behind the veil – and justice

To what would, or should, we consent concerning government, under certain hypothetical conditions, in an 'original position', a pre-government position? Note: we are now far removed from any answers automatically justifying obedience to the current state. Obedience hangs upon how close the state's features are to those receiving the relevant hypothetical consent.

Where do we start? Let us assume society's resources to lie somewhere between scarcity and abundance. Pretty obviously, if we consider individuals as if motivated by self-interest, there will be disputes. If you are already wealthy through inheritances or business, you would probably have sought a state with low taxation on inheritances and business. If you are currently ill and poor, you would be likely to promote the welfare state and taxing the wealthy. Because of such partialities, John Rawls, a highly influential twentieth-century American philosopher, argued that we need to judge how society should be from a perspective of neutrality, of impartiality – behind a 'veil of ignorance' – whereby we choose our consent, ignorant of our particular interests.

The aim behind the veil is to structure a society so that people with competing views of how life ought to be lived co-exist in reasonable harmony. That is, the aim is for a just society, for people receiving what is their due. Ignorant of our position in the society, our social status, sex, ethnicity, good or bad luck, and so forth, it would be rational to seek fair treatment for all citizens. This is Rawls' 'justice as fairness' – we might add, 'fairness through ignorance'.

Rawls extracts from under the veil a first rabbit: consent to liberty. We should seek equal freedom, autonomy, to run our lives as we want without harming others. That leads to valuing political liberty of thought and expression, free association and, indeed, ownership of personal property; but behind the veil, my consent to the utilitarian goal, for example, would be irrational for it risks my enduring significant loss, if society's overall happiness would result. We should, though, see the need for general educational and welfare provisions, and hence for lives being, to some extent, intruded upon to help others – the ill, the poor, the untalented – for we may be amongst those others.

The above stance manifests some support for luck egalitarianism (seen in Chapter Three); after all, do people *deserve* their talents, their ability to work hard and their subsequent prosperity compared to others? The response may be that they deserve the fruits of their *choices*; but arguably their choices result from their character which they did nothing to deserve. Thus we flip back to the free will puzzle. However best to handle that puzzle, Rawlsian liberalism accepts legitimate intrusions in people's lives, through redistributive taxation to help promote fairness. This receives radical rebuff from the libertarian Robert Nozick, as we shall see.

Another Rawlsian rabbit crawls from under the veil. It is the difference principle; that is, the acceptance of economic inequalities only so long as they secure the greatest benefit for the least advantaged. This is pithily summed as 'wealth inequalities justified only in as far as they maximize benefits to those with the minimum'; even more pithily, it links to a decision principle, the 'maximin'. The popular (or convenient?) empirical belief related to this is the 'trickle-down effect': resources from the wealthy trickle down to the poor, with more services being required; figuratively more butlers, more valets, more maids. Yet it may equally be argued that the greater the inequalities, the more discontent in society: the wealthy may disrespect those who have not 'made it' – who travel by bus rather than taxi – and the poor may be envious or sense themselves as failures. Those are empirical matters, but what is not empirical is whether vast wealth inequalities are, for example, morally acceptable so long as sufficient resources exist for the poorest to get by or have at least reasonable lives. There are obvious problems in assessing 'getting by' and 'reasonable' here.

Of course, some view wealth equality as possessing intrinsic value. Now, even on that view, it fails to follow that such equality must trump other values, such as liberty, or that to achieve equality we should be prepared to level everyone down. To make the point with an extreme example, if equality of resources means that none would survive, then the value of some surviving may well trump the value of equality. Witness those crash survivors with sufficient food for only one to live until rescue. Preserving at least one human life is taken as more valuable than equal shares of the food, yet no life saved.

If there are vast wealth discrepancies, yet the least well-off are flourishing, untainted by envy, then it is difficult to see any value in wealth egalitarianism. It is possible, though, that the least well-off are – from their perspective – flourishing only because they have been shielded from the greater things in life. Slaves, Muslim women in burqas, individuals blind to all values save sex and drink – they may be contented because they know no better; and, in some cases, people know no better because of poverty and upbringing – and, in other cases, because of avarice.

Suppose a society in which all are materially well-off, yet the women must never expose their ankles in public – furthermore, a certain group must always display a red star. If anyone challenges those differences, the establishment answer is 'this is what we do here; it is our tradition'. If the rules are ever put to the vote, the majority vote to maintain those rules. Even if no one complains – even if no one feels degraded by this treatment differential – is there not something offensive, assuming no good reason for it? Indeed, it may be more offensive, if certain reasons are given. 'Well, the women are women' or 'Women have periods' – or 'Well, those red-starred engage in homosexual practices.'

The above highlights an importance in equality, an importance that may be registered behind Rawls' veil. It is an equality that need not so much focus on wealth equality as on respect for people and their differences; it is sometimes promoted as 'democratic egalitarianism'.

Rawls' veil is intended as means to a rational and universal answer for what constitutes a just society, justice being assumed the key societal value. The veil, though, strips off so much from us, that we may doubt the possibility of rational motivation and assessment. Behind the veil we lack any distinctive idea of what is the good life – or, perhaps more accurately, a very thin biased conception is granted. That is, if we play the veiling game, we must choose an equal distribution of basic liberties as the primary good; but perhaps a society needs to embrace particular traditions and partialities for securing the good life. Behind the veil, some people would lose sight of certain important yet contested values concerning, for example, honour and chastity, perhaps the special role of women or the need for a holy day each week. If you believe that Allah is great, then you may be unable to subtract the belief from your motivations; and the belief would be essential to your understanding of how society should be structured.

Whichever framework is constructed by the Rawlsian method, we may wonder why that makes it rational to retain our acceptance of it now, once we do know our peculiar societal positions and beliefs about right and wrong ways of living. Present in Rawls is the impossible dream of rationality revealing the best priority of values in a society, a liberal welfare society for Rawls. True, the impossible dream is shared by others, but their reason and rationality sometimes point to a very different conclusion, a libertarian conclusion, as we shall now see via Nozick.

## Should the sighted share eyes with the blind?

Most of us possess two eyes and two kidneys. That is sheer luck. Some individuals through birth or accident are eyeless and have faulty kidneys. Suppose transplant operations were easy, reliable and painless: should a government distribute the organs more fairly? If it exercised such power – perhaps paradoxically by lottery luck – we, the former two-eyed, could retain at least one eye and one kidney each. Even with that benign retention – and supposing donors' lives are not significantly affected – few people would defend such governmental distributive powers, such 'distributive justice', even if behind Rawls' veil of ignorance. Fewer people still would defend such fairness if the donors' lives were at stake. Possession, goes the quip, is nine tenths of the law; with organ possession, it is, it seems, ten tenths. To quote John Locke:

> Though the Earth and all inferior creatures be common to all men, yet every man has a 'property' in his own 'person'. This nobody has any right to but himself.

On this view – a libertarian view – you own yourself. Self-ownership is no commitment to a metaphysical 'self'; it is an arresting way of saying that you own your body and mind, your powers and talents. With those examples, we are encouraged to accept that possession in general carries a valuation: you are entitled to your possessions – be they eyes or homemade mince pies – unless acquired by violating others. Of course, we may immediately question whether our possession of eyes is properly understood as ownership akin to that of cameras and cars.

Toiling on the land, argues Locke, is 'mixing our labour' with the land; we cultivate fruits, rear chickens or strike oil. It is wrong, unjust, to take away those laboured fruits – chickens or oil – as it is wrong, unjust, to distribute people's eyes or kidneys. The lurking assumption is that the world is initially un-owned: labour-mixing generates ownership that is just. The assumption may be questioned. Perhaps the world should be viewed as jointly owned by all; work on the world constitutes a borrowing of the material used. That challenge may harmonize with Proudhon's 'Property is theft', a slogan now with Marxist credentials, though Marx gave caveats; and even Proudhon and Marxists would enjoy private ownership of a toothbrush, underwear, even a hat.

Perhaps labour mixing allows some legitimacy to the produce, but not thereby to the land which has received the mixing. After all, if the key is that mixing something that you own with X gives you some rights to X, then a little boy who urinates in the river could end up owning the river. Even if we believe that labour-mixing generates some ownership of materials laboured upon, how extensive is that ownership? You cultivate a few fig trees; the figs ripen. Maybe that justifies your ownership of the figs, but why should it justify ownership of anything more? If it does so justify, where does it end? Does it end at the trees – at land immediately surrounding the trees – at the orchard – at the whole countryside?

Let us assume that some rightful ownership derives from the mixing. Working in the Lockean tradition, Nozick argues that what is justly mine, when voluntarily passed to others, becomes justly theirs. Thus, children's inheritances are justified and any tax attack is a violation of entitlements. It is worth noting here that

## ANNA AND BELLE: A CHALLENGE TO LIBERTARIANISM

**State of nature:** When in the state of nature, no one has the right to take over land unless 'enough and as good' is left for others – so announces Locke. Political libertarians, such as Robert Nozick, read that proviso as: any appropriation of an object must not worsen the situation of others. Presumably the proviso manifests libertarianism's concern not to intrude upon others' liberty. What, though, counts as worsening? Here is a tale:

> Anna and Belle, in a state of nature, get by, growing their own food; the result is ten smiles each. By appropriation of some local land before Belle gets to it, Anna prospers; her smiles increase to twenty. Belle now lacks access to that land – it looks as if she is worse off – but Anna offers her employment. If Belle accepts, she need be no worse-off materially: indeed, the food she receives in payment exceeds what she otherwise would have grown alone. Belle accepts the employment and, as a result, has more smiles, if based solely on material circumstances. In fact, though, Anna's land appropriation lowers Belle's overall well-being. As employee, Belle must submit to Anna's orders, experiences inequality in power, and lacks freedom to roam the land as before.

**Moral:** The moral is that if libertarians hold to the 'non-worsening' proviso, it should not be restricted solely to material conditions – and not restricted solely to those immediately affected. Why the latter consideration? Well, Belle's offspring are likely to have somewhat confined lives because of the inherited wealth of Anna's offspring. Belle's offspring will lack freedom to ramble through forests (now owned by Anna's inheritors) and maybe cannot afford good housing because inherited wealth pushes up prices. The 'non-worsening' proviso, if consistently applied, should extend to future generations – for the effective freedom of the wealthy reduces the effective freedom of the poor.

such libertarian favouring of inheritances does not justify existing wealth disparities: many disparities result from inheritances
which, if we trace back through generations, involve wealth
unjustly acquired – through battles, thefts and dubious deals.
Nozick likens most taxation to slave labour. Now, that risks exag-
geration – people are not at the mercy of the tax authorities in
the manner of slaves – but, none the less, when citizens work
some of that work is, typically, effectively unremunerated, often
against the citizens' will, for it goes in taxes. Let us see, then, how
Nozick justifies upholding wealth inequalities not generated
unjustly, and how the state, therefore, has no right to tax to provide welfare benefits and similar – an extreme 'right wing' line.

# The talented opera singer –
# the haths and hath-nots

Suppose people start off equal in wealth. Individuals possess different talents; so, suppose too that there is a remarkable opera
singer, a Maria Callas. People flock to see her. She commands vast
fees, becoming much wealthier than fellow singers and those who
buy the tickets. Voluntary transactions have taken place, violating
no one. Nothing, therefore, justifies the state taking the gains from
our Callas through redistributive taxation; thus, wealth inequalities, however great, can be justified – well, that is the argument.

Here are two quick objections. First, the taxation could be on
ticket sales before fees are received. The ticket-buying public
need not be read as saying that all ticket receipts should go to the
performers and Callas especially. Secondly, the people voluntarily
bought the tickets, but that fails to establish that they voluntarily
agreed to the resultant wealth inequalities; maybe they failed to
realize how such inequalities can generate dissatisfactions. Because
of unequal economic power the less well-off find large areas of
land prohibited to them; some cannot afford desirable housing or

good schooling for their children. The poor's liberty would be enhanced, were some wealth redistributed.

Nozick's response, based on the Kantian emphasis on respect (see previous chapter), is that wealthy individuals are then being used solely as means to a 'patterned end', a pattern pre-set of greater wealth equality; hence, those individuals are not being respected. Individuals often accept restrictions on their liberty *now* to benefit themselves in the future; but individuals *over there* may reject restrictions placed on them to benefit others *over here*. Society should not be treated as if one big unity.

The powerful libertarian principle is that however beneficial the consequences would otherwise overall be, individuals, their labour and property, should not be violated. Support for that principle is boosted by our natural repugnance at enforced eye and kidney transfers. We may wonder, though, why – according to Nozick – the autonomy of those that hath must, in all cases, take priority over correcting the reduced liberty for those that hath not. Is some amount of taxation to help the poor really akin to removing an eye to help the blind?

Nozick does accept taxation for provision of the state's and citizens' defence even, it seems, if some citizens withhold consent. That taxation provides the necessary basis for the protection and exercise of self-ownership – for, indeed, the minimal or 'night-watchman' state. With that foothold on justified taxation, perhaps taxation is also justified for welfare provision, covering risks of (even wealthy) individuals falling on hard times, and bolstering a stable society where operas occur without disruption, perhaps where talented but poor children are encouraged to develop into excellent singers.

True, with redistribution of wealth through enforced taxation, the non-consenting wealthy suffer violation of their property, but only to some extent. They may still be respected. After all, taxation levels can be set to ensure that their taxed lives are not seriously taxing and opportunities not seriously eroded. That is, support for the Kantian value of respect splinters from support for total self-ownership regarding labour and wealth. Indeed, supporting self-ownership is not thereby manifesting respect: respect involves attitudes of concern. While I may well do nothing to violate your ownership, it does not follow that I am concerned for you.

We do typically feel very differently about the state taxing our wealth and the state redistributing our eyes and kidneys. There just is, we may suggest, a clear and relevant distinction between an individual's biological extent in time and space and objects external to it. There is a big distinction between what is proper to a person being a person and the property that a person possesses. That may help to explain why a rape is typically far more horrendous than a raid on a bank account. The preservation of the integrity of an individual's biology and privacy has good claim as an essential starting point in political philosophy; yet that should not slide into viewing taxation of income and wealth as a threat to a person's integrity and respect.

Preservation of a person's integrity is at odds with dangerous and mistaken beliefs, derived from capitalist economics, that well-being is always best secured through freely operating universal markets. The repugnance typically felt towards trading bodily organs, even foetuses, for profit, paying people to befriend the lonely, buying honours, bears witness to limits on the marketable and cashable. What lies beyond those limits may be of the greatest value. Friendships, accomplishments, love and dignity are values that cannot be bought or sold without being corrupted; indeed, when within the marketplace of labour and goods, respect for individuals is required, a respect that can be lost if individuals are viewed as mere resources, consumers, cost centres or milk cows.

# The Liberty Principle

Both Rawls and Nozick take the individual as starting point; both rely on what it would be rational to accept by way of a metaphorical contract between individuals and state. Although

John Stuart Mill was no contract 'state of nature' theorist, at heart Rawls and Nozick are in accord with Mill's famous Liberty Principle, a principle met in the previous chapter:

> the only purpose for which power can be rightfully exercised over any member of a civilized community, against his will, is to prevent harm to others... Over himself, over his own body and mind, the individual is sovereign.

Note that likely harm is no sufficient condition – it is not enough – for the state to justify prohibition of activities. Maybe society, for example, is more likely to flourish with businesses in competition, despite harms resulting, when some traders are driven out of business.

Mill encouraged 'experiments in living' as contributing to flourishing lives and a flourishing society for:

> a State, which dwarfs its men, in order that they may be more docile instruments in its hands even for beneficial purposes - will find that with small men no great thing can really be accomplished...

Mill's support for liberty does not mean that all ways of living merit respect, yet, if they are not harming others, they are to be tolerated. Mill also sees that in a democracy – 'democracy' in the sense of rules determined in some way by majority votes – protection is needed against the tyranny of the majority, the tyranny of custom and, indeed, sometimes the tyranny of minority groups securing special treatment.

The Liberty Principle receives considerable discussion regarding the nature of harm and where to draw lines, whether, for example, offence counts as harm. The Principle is often criticized as highly individualistic, failing to recognize the importance of community for one's identity and values. Such importance is stressed by 'communitarians', but their position is difficult to pin down. In as far as communitarianism recognizes that what is important in people's lives can often be a sense of tradition, concern for family and friends, for 'community', then Mill's approach is not necessarily in opposition, for they can be important components of a flourishing life.

Although Rawls the liberal and Nozick the libertarian are in accord with the Liberty Principle, they use it, as seen, to travel in opposing directions. Their differences result from different orders of priorities: possession or need? That is, is the priority to be protection of what people have or is it to be that of enabling people in order to have?

ϒ

And so it is that we return to Original and Intruder on our desert island. Original, if under a libertarian political god, would not be commanded to share her goods with Intruder; yet, if under a welfarist liberal god, she would – to some extent.

Of course, on our proposed desert island, there is no political authority to determine what should be done, yet there exists the matter of what morally should be done. Now, Original may bristle at talk of 'rights' – for what rights are there in nature? She may, indeed, be a supporter of Jeremy Bentham, met in the previous chapter, who writes of natural rights as nonsense on stilts. None the less, she may have a sense of what she morally ought to do with regard to a fellow human being, with regard to Intruder, irrespective of matters of obeying a state. She may be moved by compassion, by fellow-feeling – by the Aristotelian virtues of the previous chapter – instead of insisting that what is hers is hers to keep, to keep for good or ill.

# 6
# Mind, brain and body

Inside your head, there is a brain – see what I already know about you, but knowledge is for another chapter. What is remarkable about that brain inside your head is that it is a grey slimy squelchy blob that has a lot to do with your thoughts, experiences and desires – thoughts, experiences and desires that are far from being grey, slimy and squelchy. You may be entertaining images of mermaids, memories of romantic seascapes or sensations of heat; you may be hoping to win the lottery, intending to go to the opera or deciding which dress to wear. You also possess many beliefs, motives and emotions not immediately to consciousness. Further, you could be proud, vain and in love, but unaware of such.

That slimy mess of your brain has numerous networks of gates, fibres and synapses; it has complex electro-chemical activity – yet, however deeply neurologists investigate within, they will not of course find any images at all, let alone ones of mermaids or seascapes; they will hear no sounds and spot no intentions, beliefs and yearnings. The brain, though, has something to do with all those things: cut out a portion and you may become paralysed, blind or emotionally cold. Cut out another portion and that could be the end of your short-term memory. Steamroller your brain and that is the end of you – unless immortality really is on the cards.

To avoid caveat upon caveat, when needing to refer to states or events or processes, let us often succumb to just one of those terms. Further we may, for example, speak of beliefs, leaving the

context to clarify whether the belief is to the fore of consciousness or one, a standing belief, not brought to mind. Terms
'mental' and 'psychological' are used interchangeably.

## Finding the psychological in the physical

What is the relationship between psychological states, the motley
crew mentioned – in particular, your consciousness – and that
grey slimy squelchy blob? In short, how are mind and body
related? You are in severe pain. You certainly are immediately
conscious of the pain. You are likely to groan, take painkillers,
and even risk visiting doctors. Severe pain is typically shown in
behaviour, yet there is also the immediate experience – as there
are experiences of colours and sounds and words running through
your head. Such experiences are termed *qualia*; a single is a *quale*.
Focus on the qualia, and we are tempted to view the psychological as so very different from features of brain and body.
Descartes promoted the temptation. As we saw in the first chapter, it generates a mysterious gulf between psychological states
and physical states. Further, it may enmesh us in 'other minds'
scepticism and the crazy possibility of stoical sofas: if others' pains
and thoughts are hidden, then maybe there are suffering thought-
ful subjects 'behind' the sofas.

Focus instead on what we observe of others: their behaviour.
Perhaps your happiness and thoughts about holidays just are matters of your behaviour, including linguistic behaviour, and how
you would act in certain circumstances. That is, your psychological states may in essence be your dispositions to behave in certain
ways given certain conditions. The theory – logical behaviourism –
can be understood as alerting us to what psychological states
really are (the metaphysics) *or* to what we mean when we use

psychological terms (the semantics) *or* to our criteria for telling which psychological states are present (the epistemic). The theory leads to the classic quip by a romantic behaviourist couple after lustful cavortings, 'That was great for you; how was it for me?' The metaphysical version also leads to the possibility of artificial consciousness: if robots' behaviour can be made sufficiently similar to human behaviour, then those robots must be in the same psychological states as humans, including being conscious. An immediate objection is hence the following: surely we can conceive of robots, even biological creations, which behave exactly as humans do, yet lack all experiences.

Focus, then, on the brain: popular, science-fictional and hard-headed scientific thought often treats the mind and brain as one and the same item. Think of tales of human brains removed from bodies and popped into sustaining vats, with electrodes linking the brains to eyes and voice-boxes; scientists feed the victims electro-chemical impulses causing neurological changes that determine the bad sensations or, for that matter, tingles of delight. Those tales casually, and arguably misleadingly, speak of brains thinking, imagining and intending. Perhaps we should, then, try to secure a grip on the idea that certain brain changes just are psychological changes. Schematically, experiencing a yellow blob in the imagination just is having certain neurons firing. Thus we encounter the mind–brain identity theory. The theory – as with behaviourism – is 'naturalist': understanding the psychological aright is to be in terms of the natural sciences, no reference to the supernatural or the immaterial being required.

# The mind-brain identity theory

A few decades ago, the identity theory was often known as the Australian hypothesis: it was heavily advocated by certain

Australian philosophers. It is materialist: psychological states are understood as nothing over and above states of the material world. Materialism is a monistic theory: the human being – indeed, the universe – is of one basic type: material. Materialism has been on the agenda since antiquity. These days, 'physicalism' better describes the theory for it says that the universe – including human beings – consists solely of items understood through the objective methods of, and in terms deployed by, physicists (including chemists and biologists). There is direction in the proposed identity: the psychological is 'reduced' to the physical.

The identity theory has been seen as a supplement to, and an improvement on, the behaviourism mentioned above. Consider a sugar cube that never meets water; it never dissolves, but none the less is soluble. Its solubility consists in its molecular structure – the 'categorical base' – in virtue of which it will dissolve, if immersed in water. Certain neurological structures, it is contended, are the categorical bases for different behaviours, on the occasion of certain inputs. Sensations, beliefs, intentions are nothing more than neurological states in virtue of which certain behaviour may result. Dan is in pain; the pain just is a neurological state in virtue of which, if alone, he hops and shrieks, but if with superior colleagues, he grits his teeth and keeps quiet and if with Lavinia, he asks for help – and so forth.

Both the identity theory and behaviourism find it difficult to handle qualia. It is difficult to accept that conscious experiences are literally electro-chemical neural activities; it is difficult to accept that conscious experiences are solely a matter of dispositions to behave. Indeed, in describing the possible behaviour, it seems that psychological terms must be used; in the Dan example above, 'gritting his teeth' is laden with psychology, suggestive of irritation and beliefs about how his pain ought not to be displayed.

## A THOUGHT EXPERIMENT, COURTESY OF GOTTFRIED WILHELM LEIBNIZ

Suppose that there were a machine so constructed as to produce thought, feeling, and perception. We could imagine it increased in size while retaining the same proportions, so that one could enter as one might a mill. Inside we should only see the parts impinging upon one another; we should not see anything which would explain perception. The explanation of perception must therefore be sought in a simple substance, and not in a compound or in a machine. Moreover, there is nothing else whatever to be found in the simple substance except just this, viz. perceptions and their changes.

Leibniz, *Monadology* (1714), Section 17.

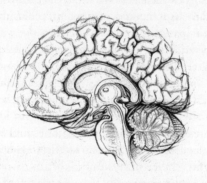

Leibniz's tale highlights that however much we investigate the brain – 'enter into the brain' – we shall remain in the dark about the mind. His metaphysical reasoning led him to an amazing conclusion. Reality consists of a plurality of indivisible soul-like entities – monads – that grounds the well-founded phenomena which form the world of physical objects. You are a monad, a rational soul; your body is appearance grounded in bare monads. Each monad is a world apart, yet represents the whole world. Courtesy of God all monads are in pre-established harmony. Leibniz claims, curiously, to be on the side of common sense.

Further, do I not possess immediate knowledge of many of my psychological states? Many are private to me; I have privileged access. In contrast, brains and behaviour are, in principle, open to public view. It is a poor joke for doctors to insist that you really are in pain, but that you fail to notice. Doctors may notice your own unnoticed injuries; but you are privileged regarding your experiences. Even if so-called MRI 'thought scans' came into use, it is difficult to see how they could trump your authority, at least for you, regarding your thoughts and sensations.

Here comes yet another problem. Apart from, for example, general depression, psychological states are directed on to things: they possess 'intentionality' (a feature brought to prominence by Franz Brentano in the nineteenth century). Your thoughts are about the stars; your memory is of the romantic assignation; your fear is directed towards the spider. Thoughts, beliefs, memories also possess content, have meaning. Your belief is that unicorns exist, that the party will be disappointing, that nineteen is a prime number. Even if behavioural dispositions may have some direction, how can they and how can neural activity possess content, possess meaning? If certain neurological events, appropriately akin to ours, were brought about in an ancient Babylonian, could that person, whatever the experiences 'from within', be thinking of digital computers and recent Afghanistan invasions? Arguably, the identity of your thoughts – indeed, the meanings of your words – partially depend on your surroundings, connections and history.

Because of the above difficulties, we may hanker after dualism, despite its own difficulties. Cartesian dualism (see Chapter One) receives little philosophical support these days; but while accepting that mind and brain are identical, some maintain that there exists a fundamental dualism of properties: the physical and the psychological. The impetus is the background belief that, through evolutionary changes, complexities arise in animal brains and, at a certain level, consciousness 'emerges'. That property dualism – a 'double aspect theory' historically associated with

Spinoza – retains a basic dualistic problem of how two radically different property types relate. Philosophers have picked up the neurologists' reports that certain fibres – for example, C-fibres – fire during mental activity; and so the philosophical puzzle schematically becomes how such firings relate to, for example, experiencing pain in the legs.

The physical causal system is often considered a closed system: changes in the physical can only be caused by other changes in the physical. If physical closure is correct, then the painfulness of the legs, understood through property dualism, has no causal role regarding the shrieking and leg clutching: the behaviour is explained solely by physical changes. That impotency of the psychological is, in fact, accepted by epiphenomenalists: according to epiphenomenalism, experiences, for example, are caused by the physical but are themselves without causal powers; they form a side-show just as, using a William James' example, the shadows that travellers cast have no effect on their travelling.

Epiphenomenalism merits incredulity. If the painfulness of pain lacks causal role in the shrieks and clutching, those actions resulting solely from relevant neurological physical changes, then presumably those changes, and hence the shrieks and leg clutching, could paradoxically have been associated with pleasures in the arms. Further, if consciousness lacks behavioural effect, it is difficult to see how it has been selected for through evolution; it must be a chance by-product. It must also be sheer luck that I typically hold correct beliefs about my psychological states, if those beliefs are just by-products, lucky shadows, of physical changes.

## Losing the mind

The implausibility of epiphenomenalism returns us to the identity theory: psychological events just are neural firings that, in the case of pains, may cause further electro-chemical changes that cause shrieks and clutching. Recall of Leibniz's Indiscernibility of Identicals (encountered in Chapter One) will remind us of some perplexities for the identity theory.

If seemingly two items are in fact identical, then, with certain caveats, everything true of one must be true of the other. Truths concerning neurological happenings refer to physical locations, electro intensity and chemical levels. If certain neurological states just are my musings, memories and hopes, then those psychological states must also have physical location, electro intensity and so forth. Does it, though, make sense to speak of a hope being one inch in from the left ear? For that matter, does it make sense to speak of a neurological state as being 'about' or 'directed on', for example, success in forthcoming examinations?

Eliminative materialism, the 'disappearance theory of mind', offers a robust answer. In arguable summary, it urges, 'Just don't say those things: drop the old terms'. Our talk of sensations, thoughts and beliefs deploys concepts of a long-standing theory that seeks to explain human behaviour: the theory is dubbed 'folk psychology'. Evidence is coming our way that suggests the theory needs replacement. Folk psychology, it is predicted – and it is just a prediction – will give way to neurological explanations of behaviour, explanations that may well jettison many of our current psychological terms. Here is an analogy.

Scientists once held that burning consisted of a noble substance, phlogiston, being released into the air. The phlogiston theory was replaced by the oxygen theory; the concept of 'phlogiston' was junked. Disturbed people used to be possessed by devils with malicious intent – well, so it was believed. In civilized countries, the devil theory has been dropped (in the main); instead there are neurological explanations and interventions. No one seriously thinks that an objection to neurological explanations of disturbed behaviour is their lack of reference to devils with malicious intent. We do not anguish about how chemical levels could have malicious purposes or be cunning spirits.

Reference to devils was reference to theoretical entities: the theory is jettisoned and so are the entities.

In similar vein to the above, recommend eliminativists, let us not worry that neurological activity cannot be understood as possessing qualia or intentionality. As our neurological understandings develop, we may well discard those old psychological concepts – and live in a clear-thinking new world of neurological explanations. True, we may still use the old words – but, then, we talk of the sun rising, when really we know it is the Earth moving.

The brave stance of eliminativists deserves full marks for implausibility. After all, it is far from clear that our understanding of others in folk psychological terms is defective. We do pretty well in predicting people's behaviour. Additionally, there is something inescapable about concepts such as belief, sensation, hope and desire. They do not present as theoretical entities; we experience sensations, thoughts *et al* directly. Certainly, they cannot be easily dismissed from our conceptual scheme – in contrast to phlogiston and devil possession.

Assuming we retain our current psychological concepts, maybe we could still acquire a scientific understanding of them. After all, stimulate the brain in certain areas and patients (or victims) experience certain types of sensation. That is evidence for psychological changes being neurological. Note, though, that even if the tingles occur when and only when those fibres are firing, that fails to establish the tingles and firings as identical. They may be correlated, one causing the other; so dualism is not refuted by such evidence. Bring forth Ockham's Razor.

Ockham, a medieval logician – more accurately, his pupils – offered the following methodological principle: entities ought not to be multiplied beyond necessity. Psychological states, if taken as additional to the physical, are sent to the barbers and cut away. Give neurologists time, and the brain will be mapped, showing which firings *et al* are which psychological states. There are resultant dangers; they need to be guarded against.

If having pains and memories just is being in certain types of neurological states, then it looks as if, of logical necessity, we are ruling out octopuses, whales and aliens having pains and memories. Surely creatures with radically different internal structures, lacking human or even neurological types of structure, may yet be conscious, with pains, pleasures, memories and the like.

Identity theorists can avoid the above homo-bio-prejudice, the chauvinism; and the avoidance brings further advantages. To show how, we introduce the type/token distinction. 'How many beers were served today?' You could read that in terms of types – perhaps five types were served – or read it regarding pints, instances or tokens of those five types. Perhaps twenty beers of each type were served, making one hundred tokens in total.

Now, some identity theorists maintain that types of psychological events reduce to types of neural events. That type-type theory is exposed to the chauvinism complaint just made. In contrast, the token-token theory simply claims that any psychological event just is a physical event, but there is no necessity for the same type of psychological event to be the same type of physical event: there are no laws linking psychological concepts to the neurological. Although the pains in humans, in octopuses, in aliens, are all physical events, they are not thereby all the same type of physical event – even though they are all the same type of psychological event. A question immediately arises: why, then, do they all count as pains? That returns us to a focus on the associated behaviour.

## Back to behavioural basics

We are neither born aware of linguistic meanings nor lucky recipients of magical learning. We develop language from infancy with people using terms such as 'pain', 'thinking' and 'remembering' of us, when we behave in certain ways; we pick up such uses.

Grasp of the meaning of those psychological terms involves grasp of associated behaviour: 'meaning is use'.

The woman thinking of England is disposed to utter words about England, but maybe she will utter them only if asked and in certain circumstances. Those circumstances involve reference to other psychological states, whether she *wants* to speak, whether she *feels* embarrassed and so forth. Awareness of the complex web of psychological states relating to potential behaviour has led to recent support for 'functionalism'. The approach is but sophisticated behaviourism. Psychological states, according to functionalism, are complex functions and functions are causal roles.

Let us focus first on psychological states involving thoughts, intelligence and understanding, then more directly on qualia.

Alan Turing – yes, he of computer fame and who led the team that cracked the Enigma Code in World War II – suggested a test, the Turing Test, for whether there could be artificial intelligence, whether a machine could be 'minded'. The test is in the spirit of functionalism. Suppose a machine (a robot, a computer) with perfect human speaking devices is hidden from view – as is also a human. If interrogators, by simply asking the same questions of both hidden machine and hidden human, cannot tell whether they are in dialogue with the machine or human, then the machine is as intelligent as the human. Of course, sufficiently wide-ranging questions need to be asked (not, for example, just concerning mathematical calculations) and the machine needs to be programmed to provide sufficient human foibles – the 'er's, 'y'knows' *et al*. Let us use some analogies to see the consequence of this view.

A piece is a knight in the game of chess when it plays a certain role. One chess-set may have wooden pieces, another set ceramic, yet another, pixels on screen. What is essential is the knightly role, not the stuff which composes the piece. Similar comments may be made about clocks and weapons, and – drawing closer to psychological home – banks' answering systems may consist of digital automation, old-fashioned tapes or living employees, desperate for work, in far-off lands. The above illustrates how certain roles or states with a readiness to respond may be multiply realizable. So too are psychological states, according to functionalists, thus avoiding the bio-chauvinism of traditional identity theories. The mind, speaking casually, is akin to a programme that may run on different hardware or biological wetware. Our psychological states are causal roles manifested by neural firings that can affect human bodies; those same psychological states, though, do not have to be manifested in neural firings. Perhaps the causal roles could have been played by changes in the heart, by circuits of silicone chips, or even outlandish spiritual items. Thus, octopuses, even aliens of different solar systems, may have pains just as we do, if they have internal systems with sufficiently similar causal or functional structures. Thus it is that functionalism is compatible with token-token identity theories, though it does not thereby, of course, solve the puzzle of how physical states give rise to intentionality and qualia.

We should, in fact, distinguish between roles and realizers. With the chess example, we spoke of the knight being the role, yet we may think of the knight as this particular piece but only because it realizes that role. So psychological states here are sometimes understood as the role played, but sometimes as the items that realize the role – but those items are psychological solely because they do realize those roles.

In contrast to the chauvinism threat, functionalism runs the danger of excess liberalism. The dangers are typically exposed via certain thought experiments, such as those from contemporary American philosophers, John Searle and Ned Block (please see insert over the page). Searle's Chinese Room, directed at the Turing Test's liberalism, is designed to show that although there is the right function with the right outputs for understanding, understanding is absent. Block's China Brain focuses on the qualia problem.

**PSYCHO-SINOLOGY AND FUNCTIONALISM**

# The Chinese Room

In a closed room sits an English speaker, ignorant of Chinese, surrounded by slips of paper with Chinese characters: they could be double-dutch as far as he knows. Chinese speakers outside the room post him slips of Chinese characters, 'invites', which need replies. He possesses a complicated rule book, in English, which tells him which Chinese characters to use in which order, depending upon the invites' characters and order. Invites arrive; he dishes out replies according to the rule book. Perhaps the invites are factual questions about geography. The replies are appropriate.

What is clear – at least to John Searle, the originator – is that the room-bound person, although ignorant of Chinese, functions such that Chinese outsiders would think that he understands Chinese. The room-bound man handles the syntax, the Chinese characters, but lacks grasp of what is meant, the semantics. Successful symbol manipulation is insufficient for understanding.

Searle insists that the same moral should be drawn if the man memorized the rule book, churning out responses through vocal chords instead of on paper.

# The China Brain

Neural activity consists, apparently, of electrical impulses in certain causal configurations. Suppose there is a brainless artificial body, Art, the substitute for his brain being the billion Chinese people playing the causal roles that a brain would play. The people have the right wireless causal links to Art's body.

Art has sensors. When Art's toe is hit, signals go to certain Chinese players' receivers and they, according to a schedule, send impulses to others. Those processes lead to further signals between players which lead to signals to Art's body causing shrieks and the words 'Stop that!' The Chinese players are not suffering and shrieking.

The right causal roles are in play, so functionalists should accept the counterintuitive claim that Art has pains in the toe. That is, the Chinese nation's configuration of firings just is the experience of toe pain. True, depending on the radio transmissions, Art may not respond as speedily as typical humans do when toes are hit.

In the spirit of Searle's thought experiment, outlined on the previous page, but at a more basic level, burglar alarms behave according to the environment; but we have no inclination to consider the alarms intelligent or, for that matter, psychologically dumb. The alarms do not muse upon external movements, with desires to alert. A response is that humans differ from alarms and Searle's room-bound individual; humans possess understanding because of more highly developed complexity. Certain properties can emerge from complexity: piles of sand remain static until a stage is reached when additional grains lead to avalanches. That there are such emergent examples does not, of course, establish that, as a result of neurological causal complexity, psychological states also emerge.

Time, now, for the qualia problem – with the Sino-experiment where members of the Chinese nation send signals to each other, as if constituting the transmitters and receptors of a brain, hooked to an artificial body. The functional connections being in the right array, functionalists should accept that some qualia are present to the artificial body – to Art, as described on the previous page – yet is not that highly counter-intuitive?

The China brain strikes many as all too outlandish or vague, with casual talk of neural firings as Chinese signallings, yet we may reach its heart by a different route, one which may lose the 'counterintuitive' accolade – well, for a while.


# Regular Reg – zombies and bats

Suppose we have a regular human being – Reg – with typical conscious experiences. If the functionalist view (or, for that matter, the identity view) is correct, then there is nothing special about the brain's headed location. We could conceive of the brain outside the head, with standard connections and configurations intact, though perhaps stretched. Reg could even carry his brain wherever he goes within a resistant leak-free knapsack containing suitable nutrients. There is, it seems, nothing theoretically impossible about that scenario, though, true, Reg's movements may be restricted.

To avoid mobility constraints, let there be wireless connections between Reg's brain and the rest of his body – and now the knapsack with brain can be left in a luggage locker while Reg's body sallies forth. After all, it matters not at all to the brain how the inputs from Reg's skin, eyes, ears *et al* arrive.

With wireless links between brain and body, we could develop our thought experiment: we could gradually replace the fibre connections within the brain itself with wireless impulses, while ensuring the same configuration remains. Let us go further still: we could spread the brain's transmitters and receivers across the universe, while maintaining the relevant configuration of impulses. Despite those changes, we have no good reason, on functionalist grounds, for supposing that Reg suddenly lacks experiences. Reg's body – its movements and vocal outputs – continue in the regular way.

What holds things together, so to speak, for Reg's psychology is the set of linkages, albeit wireless, to Reg's body; yet Reg's body may not even be required if we hold firm to the functionalist approach. If functionalists think of causal roles alone as determining experiences – well, those roles and neurological realizers of those roles exist 'doing their thing', even if lacking successful external bodily effects. After all, the structure of causal impulses and states that, according to functionalist theory, constitute the experiences of seeing a cat or having pains in the toe could exist with neither cat as cause nor foot. Consider the following analogy.

A thermostat's innards could be working properly, yet if not connected to a regular boiler or if connected to a rogue boiler, the thermostat fails to maintain the required temperature. For a further consideration, the relevant changes *within* the thermostat just need reliably to occur in sequences, without one actually causing the other, if causal relations are in fact more than regular conjunctions of events. Indeed, if psychological states are temporal patterns of neural firings, then consider the trillions of such firings occurring at this very moment because of the billions of people in existence. Those trillions, spread across billions of people, are likely to be in various relevant patterns which, if causation is nothing more than regular patterning, may be constitutive of numerous psychological experiences, though lacking appropriate connections to bodies.

$$\gamma$$

The seas of philosophical reasoning can be rough; we may drown in absurd speculations. Things have gone wrong if we take seriously the claim that psychological states need just patterns, be they of neurological firings or impulses in silicon chips. Perhaps certain biological properties – perhaps spatial relations – are essential for the psychology. After all, Beethoven's Ninth Symphony would lose its beauty and effect, were the separate notes playing miles away from each other and on tin cans.

In truth, the mind-body problem haunts philosophers, whatever degree of confidence some express by way of solution – or confidence that the problem is bound to be a mystery for human beings: the 'mysterium' view. Theories try to reduce psychological states to something else – to neural configurations, behaviour, or causal roles. Perhaps the correct response is a general one from the eighteenth-century Bishop Joseph Butler: everything is what it is and not another thing.

Let us not lose sight of the direct importance of the human body, the animal, and its surroundings, when swept along by thought experimental speculations.

We do not seriously think that sofas could be in pain: there is nothing that sofas do, expressive of pain; there is nothing that sofas need that could be the source of pain.

Were we to string certain neural firings together in a petri dish, do we really believe that thereby we have created the thought that, for example, Plato was a great philosopher? Arguably, thoughts, beliefs, hopes and desires need embodiment, and also appropriate surroundings and encounters.

The psychological, we suggest, presupposes capacities to express – capacities currently manifested solely by certain biological creatures – and those capacities require worldly engagements. True, there are cases of 'locked-in' syndrome, of people now unable to express much or anything at all, but we ought not to ignore the history of those cases. Just because huge misfortunes are possible for individuals already with acquired concepts of human living, it does not follow that they are possible for entities without that prior living and learning.

Perhaps it is a mistake to decompose human activities into psychological and physical components. Lori is riding a bicycle, flirting with her colleague, preparing for a concert that evening, ready to sign a mortgage contract tomorrow; such mishmashes of human activities are enmeshments of the psychological and physical, not readily separable into so many psychological elements, so many physical ones. If Lori is happy, she may smile in appropriate circumstances – but human smiling is not composed solely of facial changes. Our thoughts, feelings and desires – our psychology – engage a fleshy life: coaxing lovers with headaches, using chairs as coat-hangers, making promises, fuming at the music's loudness and at the perpetrator's lack of courtesy.

Contrast 'intelligent' computers stuck in corners – or clanking, even smooth-travelling, robots – with embodied human beings rushing across the beach, trying not to drop the ice-creams, yelling at the children, glancing at the lithe sunbathers and eager for a swim. Knowing how to handle things in the human world is essential for our concept possession. The robots and speculative modifications to humans would need such forms of life to merit any sense-filled ascriptions of psychology.

♈

'If a lion could talk, we could not understand him,' wrote Wittgenstein. Quips apart that if the lion says 'I'm hungry' we may dash for protection, we can see how the lion's world, interests and needs, are largely alien to the world of human beings – yet only 'largely'. There are some basic similarities: for example, hunger, pain, sexual arousal. We have no grip regarding such matters with the sofa – and no grip of lions understanding career development, banking crises or consumerism. Wittgenstein anguished much about how to understand the psychological. He is reported as saying:

> A person caught in a philosophical confusion is like a man in a room who wants to get out but doesn't know how. He tries the window but it is too high. He tries the chimney but it is too narrow.

The room still entraps. However hard we seek escape, we may yet be struck by the sheer conceivability of the philosophers' zombies, of human-like behaviour unlinked to any experiences – or of 'super-stoics' whose pains are never manifested outwardly, or 'super-shammers' whose behaviour radically misleads. Thus, we may collapse in the room of confusion, of bafflement, when we muse upon the now famous philosophical question, 'What is it like to be a bat?'

However much we may learn about the bat's echo system, however much we may examine the bat's neural structures –

whatever flights of fancy we may engage, when hanging upside down from the chapel's rafters flapping our arms – we may still feel that there is something forever elusive: namely, the bat's consciousness, its perspective on the world.

What, indeed, is it like to be a bat?

Even if bats could talk, we could not understand them.

# 7

# What, then, is knowledge?

'Do you know the way to San José?' The local standing at the crossroads points straight ahead. You trek off in the indicated direction and, sure enough, you reach San José. All is well; the man had not misled you. 'Ah,' says the philosopher, 'but did he *know* the way?'

Sceptical philosophers question virtually all claims to knowledge; they cast doubt on the possibility of knowledge. We shall assess their arguments in the next chapter, but it is no bad thing to secure a grip on what knowledge is before assessing scepticism. After all, before assessing whether unicorns exist, we need knowledge of what a unicorn is – and certainly in everyday life we recognize that some people are possessors of knowledge, others not. So, did the local know the way to San José?

Knowledge has frequently been understood in terms of necessary and sufficient conditions. Here is a quick model – that of a geometrical figure being a square. One necessary condition is that the figure has four sides, but four sides are insufficient: a four-sided figure could be highly irregular and very un-squared. We can, though, build up conditions – a four-sided closed figure, sides equal in length, internal angles being right angles – conditions which jointly are sufficient for any figure being a square. With that simple example in mind, what conditions are necessary for someone to know that Stockholm is the capital of Sweden, that tomorrow is Aunt Matilda's birthday, and that heading straight is the way to San José? More generally, what conditions need to be fulfilled for you to know that $p$ – where '$p$' is a marker for propositions or claims or statements such as those mentioned?

If you know that $p$, then it follows that $p$ is true. No one can know that Paris is the capital of France, if it is not. Truth is one necessary condition for knowledge; but that a proposition is true is not sufficient for anyone to know that truth. There is the truth of how many polar bears are sitting within the Arctic Circle right now, yet no one knows that truth – not even the polar bears. Consider a truth known to some people – for example, that the President drank champagne at breakfast today. For you and I to know that to be so, not merely must there be the truth of the matter, but we need to think – believe, affirm, be certain – that he drank champagne today. A necessary condition for people to know that $p$, in addition to $p$'s truth, is that they are in a certain type of psychological state concerning the proposition's truth. For simplicity, that state is typically treated as one of belief – belief understood such that it does not thereby rule out knowledge. Let us here speak of the relevant psychological condition as belief.

True belief is necessary for knowledge, but is it sufficient? The traditional answer is 'no'. A true belief may be nothing more than a lucky guess, a groundless conviction. You wake up one morning, strangely convinced that the horse Lady Godiva will win at Ascot tomorrow. Furthermore, you are right; you hit lucky. Yet it is implausible to insist that you knew that Lady G would win: more is required. The 'more' has often been presented as your belief being justified. You need, it is suggested, some evidence, some reason, some warrant – some justification – to rule out your belief being sheer luck. Evidence, in this example, could be your determination to feed sleeping pills to the competing runners.

Thus, for example, it has been proposed that Oscar knows that $p$ if and only if:

   (i)   '*p*' is true;
   (ii)  Oscar believes that *p*;
   (iii)  Oscar is justified in his belief that *p*.

In the above, (i) is a necessary condition for knowledge. Why? Well, only if '*p*' is true does Oscar know that *p*. Similarly, (ii) and (iii) are each necessary conditions. Taken jointly (i), (ii) and (iii) are sufficient for Oscar to know that *p* – well, according to this tripartite analysis, knowledge as true justified belief.

The analysis is traditional: arguably, it derives from Socrates' insistence that knowledge only exists when the relevant beliefs are stable – when the beliefs are tethered to the believers, not through stubbornness or obsession, but as a result of their truth. As a teeny tribute to Socrates, let the stability ingredient be deemed a tethering. Your ability to provide justification – reason, evidence – for a belief's truth tethers you to that truth. If you have good reasons for what you believe, then it should not be that easy for others to persuade you from your belief: you can put up a defence for the truth of your belief.

We shall shortly see a different arena – one external to the mind – for the tethering; but, for the moment, we continue in traditional mode. The analysis's justification condition is internal to the knowers' psychology. It is what knowers – perhaps when challenged – offer as reasons for their proclaimed knowledge or, at least, what they can offer, after reflection.

The motivation, as suggested, behind the tethering proposal is that, when we know – for example, that Plato wrote the *Meno* – our belief that he did should hold firm if people suggest otherwise. One problem is: how firm? Our beliefs, even when with excellent reasons, are not thereby true; and so, unwittingly, we may have bound ourselves to falsity. To avoid error and dogmatism, we need some readiness to expose our beliefs to counter-evidence and counter-arguments. There results the following

## THE STATUES OF DAEDALUS – TETHERING

The Daedalus tale is told by Socrates, according to Plato's account in his early dialogue *Meno*. Socrates and Meno are discussing knowledge. Meno points out that when people hold true beliefs – right opinions – all is well. They have the truth; so why is knowledge more prized, thought more valuable? In wanting to know the San José way, you simply want the truth. Socrates offers to explain – unless Meno already 'knows' the answer. Thus we encounter a touch of Socratic wit: even the greatest of philosophers – and the lowliest – may possess dubious humour. Socrates notes that perhaps Meno is unaware of the fine sculptor Daedalus and his statues which are so very lifelike:

> If no one ties down his statues, they run away and escape; but, if tied, they stay where they are put. So, if you have one of his works untethered, it is not worth much; it gives you the slip like a runaway slave. A tethered specimen, though, is very valuable for they are magnificent creations.

That, says Socrates – to Meno's initial bewilderment – has a bearing on true beliefs:

> True beliefs are a fine thing and do all sorts of good as long as they stay in their place; but they will not stay long. They run away from a man's mind, so they are not worth much until you tether them by working out the reason.

Possessing justifications for your beliefs is a means of holding your beliefs firm, of stabilizing them such that they constitute knowledge and not lucky guesses.

paradoxical thought and hence danger: if we really do know that $p$, then ought we not to know that any evidence against $p$ is misleading – and hence reject it? We leave that puzzle for some musing, related matters appear in the following chapter; here, we turn to another problem.

That knowers must possess reasons for holding their beliefs gives rise to the thought that those reasons must also be known – and thus they would need sustaining with yet further reasons. I believe that Quito is the capital of Ecuador, my reason being the testimony of maps; but, in order for that belief to be knowledge, I surely must possess reasons for believing that the maps are reliable, that my eyesight is good and so forth. That consideration may lead us to conclude that knowledge must ultimately rest on foundations in need of no further reasons. The foundations, some have argued, must be our immediate experiences or certain basic beliefs over which we are 'right to be sure'.

If it is accepted that we possess knowledge of knowledge's foundations, then that foundational knowledge fails the analysis of knowledge as true *justified* belief. Hence, instead of appeals to foundations, some stress the need for beliefs to cohere within a comprehensive web of beliefs. A coherent and comprehensive web, though, may be a web of mutually supportive falsehoods: coherence alone does not secure truth.

The concerns just mentioned move us towards problems of scepticism, deferred until the next chapter. Here, our philosophic focus returns to knowledge's traditional analysis.

## Camilla, Cassandra and confusions

The traditional analysis is open to two types of challenge. The first raises the question: are the three components each in fact necessary for knowledge? The second is: are the three components, taken jointly, sufficient for knowledge? The challenges have usually led to modifications, supplementations or re-interpretations of the traditional analysis rather than outright rejection.

Looking at the proposed necessary conditions, the truth requirement, although sometimes generating muddles, is rarely doubted, except by those who bizarrely deny the existence of truth or truths. The belief and justification conditions, though, have suffered many objections. Here is a typical apparent counter-example to the belief requirement.

Circumstances may be such that nervous candidates at interviews, overwhelmed with anxiety or aggressive questioning, have mental blanks or are unsure what they believe; consequently, they fail to provide correct answers. May they not – contrary to the traditional analysis – none the less *know* the answers? Before the interviews, they readily give voice to their beliefs, manifesting knowledge, and afterwards, likewise. Camilla, in the calmness of classroom (yes, an unusual school), knows Boyle's Law, can explain it and the evidence for it, yet pop her in a competitive interview for a university place and she collapses into burbles.

A quick response to Camilla's burbles is that, in those circumstances, she is unable to express the required beliefs, not that she lacks those beliefs. Neither beliefs nor knowledge need be immediately accessible to consciousness. When asleep, we are in no position to give voice to our beliefs and knowledge, yet it would be odd to insist that sleep eradicates our beliefs and knowledge, with those same beliefs and the knowledge magically returning when we awake. So, even when we are awake and able to reflect, perhaps external pressures can be so oppressive – making us anxious, confused and nervous – that we can neither access certain knowledge and beliefs nor express them.

Similar challenges and similar responses can be made with regard to knowers' ability to give reasons for their beliefs. Circumstances may be such that, during interviews, some candidates provide the right answers, but are so nervous that they are unable to justify their answers. We may still consider that they possess reasons – and maybe knowledge – but are unable to voice them.

Those examples bring to light an important distinction, one easily overlooked with resultant error about the conditions for knowledge. The distinction is shown by two questions. What constitutes knowledge? When is someone justified in claiming to have knowledge? Many subtleties arise; here is some minimal groundwork. It may be reasonable and appropriate for me to claim 'I know that she finished the whisky last night,' yet – as it transpires – I am mistaken: she did not. We can rightly say of Camilla that she knows Boyle's Law, even though, because of her uncertainty, she may be right not to claim such knowledge for herself.

It is easy to confuse what is required for someone to be justified in making a knowledge claim with what is required for that individual to possess the knowledge in question. What we may be justified in saying about what Camilla knows may be something that she would not be justified in saying about herself. A famous paradox – Moore's Paradox – rests on cases where what we may say of someone else without absurdity can be said by that person of herself only with absurdity. It may be true that today is Sunday, yet you believe it is Monday. I can say that of you, yet if you say it about yourself – 'Today is Sunday, but I believe it is Monday' – it is absurd.

To see the value of the distinction between possessing knowledge and being justified in claiming to possess knowledge, let us turn to another counter-example to the traditional analysis with regard to knowledge's necessary conditions. Some have argued that, even ignoring foundational beliefs, people may know that $p$ – and firmly believe that $p$ – despite lacking reasons, evidence or grounds, and not because of odd surroundings that prevent their recognition of their beliefs and reasons.

Cassandra awakes one morning, convinced that it will rain that afternoon. She can offer no reasons, yet – as it weatherly transpires – she is right. On the surface that was mere luck. Suppose, though, that Cassandra is consistently right; and she predicts rain when and only when it does then rain. After a long run of success, we should surely turn to Cassandra for

## KNOWLEDGE: HANDLE WITH CARE

# The truth requirement

'If Oscar knows that p, then p must be true.' The claim is ambiguous between the following:

> If Oscar knows that p, then it necessarily follows that 'p' is true.
> If Oscar knows that p, then it follows that 'p' is necessarily true.

The latter permits knowledge solely of necessary truths; yet our use of 'know' does not confine knowledge in that way. We know – well, so it seems – a vast number of contingent truths, truths that just happen to be true. You know you are reading this book, but that is not a necessary truth – for you might not have been reading this book.

# The safety of necessary truths?

'Believe only necessary truths – to avoid error.' That thought mis-locates the error danger; after all, so long as we believed only truths of whatever kind, we should be avoiding error. Our reasoning and the evidence may mislead us not solely over contingent truths, but also over necessary truths. Think of the mathematical mistakes we make, yet mathematics concerns necessary truths.

# The 'not being mistaken' fallacy

'If you know, then you cannot be mistaken.' Is that true?

You have excellent evidence that Jesse is drinking whisky: you can see her; she regularly drinks whisky; glass is in her hand and so forth. None the less it may transpire that you are wrong – even though in fact it does not so transpire. If it does transpire that you are wrong – and it may – then you lack knowledge of her drinking whisky: you merely think that you know. Knowledge requires that you are not mistaken, but not that you cannot be mistaken.

weather forecasts. She knows, even though she possesses no reasons for her predictive beliefs: she does not know how she knows. We now rely on Cassandra's forecasts because of her prior successes; but her continuing predictive beliefs may not be grounded in those past successes. Because of her continuing success, we may reflect that even the earlier successes were instances of knowledge. We may be led to the following reflection.

There must be an appropriate causal link between her belief and what makes the belief true. Perhaps Cassandra is sensitive to atmospheric pressure which both accounts for her belief and is causally involved in the afternoon rain. That causal link may be unknown to Cassandra and to us. Although she claimed on the first occasion 'I just know it', she may not have been justified in making her claim. The causal link may have been sufficient, though, for her to possess the knowledge in question. Thus, knowledge's justification condition need not require knowers to have reasons; the condition can be satisfied, it seems, by a relevant causal link – by an external factor unknown to her.

The above example brings to the fore how the tethering metaphor may apply in two distinct ways. Being able to give reasons for $p$, to stabilize or tether your belief that $p$, is directly relevant to whether you are justified in claiming to know that $p$. However, whether you do know, or not, depends on whether your belief is appropriately tethered to what makes the belief true. Now, good reasons, as well as stabilizing your belief, may tether your belief to the truth; an appropriate causal link, unknown to you, may, though, also be sufficient by way of tether.

The focus on causation has led to analyses of knowledge in which the appropriate causal links are essential: the knowers' reasons are only relevant in that they may manifest the links. The causal approach, let us add, is no quick solution to our understanding knowledge, for how can abstract truths such as those of pure mathematics have causal impact – how can numbers be causes? Even with empirical beliefs, we have the problem that the analysis of causation is as difficult as that of knowledge. Philosophers often think they have sorted out a murky conceptual mess here – only to find it has been brushed under the carpet to over there.

## Harry Hawk-eyed

The observations above concern the necessary conditions for knowledge. Time to turn to attacks on the proposal that true justified belief is sufficient for knowledge. The attacks present counter-examples, examples designed to establish that there can be cases where people have true justified beliefs, yet (it seems) lack knowledge. The counter-examples are often deemed to be Gettier-type examples, so-named because of Edmund Gettier's paper, famed for its brevity as well as its challenge. The underlying consideration can be traced to Bertrand Russell decades earlier. Let us set a scene with Harry. We initially focus on knowledge where the justification consists in the good reasons that the (seeming) knower can provide.

Hawk-eyed Harry keeps his hawk eye trained each morning upon all who walk down the sole path to his private beach. He firmly believes that someone is on the beach right now; his belief is true: someone is, namely Suzie. His belief is appropriately tethered for he has excellent reasons. 'I've been watching carefully and I saw Suzie go by, as usual, with towel, book and suntan cream – and she has not yet returned.' He is right to claim that he knows – and he does know. Here now comes a Gettier-type example, with the above scenario modified.

Hawk-eyed Harry has indeed spied Suzie swaying down the cliff's sole path to the secluded beach to sunbathe. He now believes that Suzie is sunbathing and, being something of a logician, he concludes that therefore *someone* is sunbathing on that beach. If you are willing to bet that Suzie is sunbathing, you surely should be willing to bet that someone is sunbathing. The Gettier-type puzzle arises because of the following new elements to the example.

The important element is that someone is indeed sunbathing on the beach, yet it is not Suzie, but a woman unknown to Harry. It is Rugged Ruth who clambered down rocks, unseen by Harry, to reach the golden but private sands. Suzie has succumbed to the temptations of a millionaire's yacht, love and champagne; she has been whisked away. Still, Harry's belief that *someone* is sunbathing is true. Further, his belief is tethered: the proposition that someone is sunbathing logically follows from the proposition that Suzie is sunbathing and his belief in the latter is justified because he saw Suzie go down, with towel, suntan cream and similar. Harry, it seems, has a true and justified belief, yet – we probably feel – he does not know that someone is sunbathing. It is sheer luck that his belief that someone sunbathes there is true. Yet, on the surface at least, it was reasonable for him to claim to know.

What is to be done?

Harry's justification includes a false step – namely that Suzie is sunbathing – so an obvious revision to the justification condition for what constitutes knowledge, when by way of reasons, is that the reasoning must include no false steps. That insistence, though, is pretty inadequate. After all, Harry saw someone (namely, Suzie) walking down and he could have concluded straight off, without false steps, that someone would be sunbathing. A response to that is as follows. Were Harry to construct the reasoning to justify his belief that someone is sunbathing, the false Suzie belief would come to the fore as essential. If that response is adequate, we may be led to the unhappy and excessively strong conclusion that we can never be justified in holding a belief that, as it transpires, turns out to be false. Perhaps the correct conclusion, though, is that a justification with an unknown false step undermines the fact that someone knows, without thereby making the claim to knowledge unreasonable or unjustified.

One way of tackling what is going on here is to focus on the weakness of the tether, the instability of Harry's belief that someone is sunbathing on the beach. The weakness is shown thus:

> If Harry discovered that Suzie was not sunbathing on the beach –
> perhaps she telephones him from the yacht – then he would no
> longer be sure that someone was sunbathing there, even though
> it would be true that someone was sunbathing there.

His reasons for his 'someone' belief is defeasible: that is, Harry would no longer hold his true belief, were he to encounter some further information – in this case, that Suzie romances on a millionaire's yacht. His reasons and belief would be defeated.

The above consideration leads to the following supplementation to knowledge's traditional analysis: the analysis's justification must be one that is *indefeasible*. For knowledge to exist – perhaps, even, for knowledge claims to be justified – the justification by way of reasons must not be open to defeat by evidence which happens not to be possessed – in this case, it is the evidence that Suzie is not sunbathing. Were Harry to encounter that evidence, he would no longer maintain his belief that someone is sunbathing. His 'someone' belief lacks appropriate tethering; it can readily fall away from the truth that someone is sunbathing and also can run away from Harry's mind, if faced with the new evidence.

At this point, we may welcome the causal relation as the key regarding the nature of knowledge. What leads Harry to his belief that someone is sunbathing is Suzie swaying down the cliff's path; but Suzie has nothing to do with the truth of Harry's 'someone' belief. The causal explanation of Harry's 'someone' belief contains no reference to causal transactions that led to his 'someone' belief being true. What makes Harry's 'someone' belief true – namely, Ruth's sunbathing – lacks relevance regarding the source of Harry's 'someone' belief.

The above shows that the causal analysis of knowledge would not be open to the Gettier-type example just discussed. All, though, is not well for the causal analysis.

All is not well, for fresh Gettier-type examples exist that pose problems for the tethering involved in knowledge, whether it be understood as a causal link or the apparent knowers possessing good reasons involving no false steps or that are indefeasible. Here come two examples.

## Discriminations

Harry is a keen bird watcher. At his look-out post, he correctly informs us that there is a seagull opposite. On the analyses discussed, by way of his possession of reasons and the existence of an appropriate causal link, he knows that there is a seagull. That is because he believes it to be a seagull; it is a seagull – and he is seeing it right now, in the clear light of day. Hence, his visual experiences provide him with excellent justification for his belief; indeed, that very seagull figures in the causal explanation of his belief. Suppose, though, that we later observe his gazing at a kestrel, then an eagle – and he says perfectly seriously and with confidence, 'Ah, there's another seagull – and another.' That would surely show that he lacked knowledge that there was a seagull in the first place, even though he was able to justify his initial belief and there existed an appropriate causal link. It is

Harry's unreliability as seagull spotter that shows his lack of knowledge with regard to bird identification – and such lack makes inappropriate his claim that he knew he had seen a seagull. Note that his initial seagull belief fails as knowledge even if Harry sees no other birds and hence in fact makes no further misidentifications. All that is required is the truth of the following counterfactual: had Harry seen some non-seagulls, such as kestrels and eagles, he would have mistaken them for seagulls. Here, we edge towards the thought that knowledge requires reliability, requires an *ability* to discriminate between relevant cases – whether or not circumstances arise to manifest that ability. After all, this sugar cube is soluble – and that is true, even if it never encounters water or similar, and so, never dissolves. We turn to our second example.

Harry knows Suzie well. A woman walks by, heading for the beach; he has no doubt that she is Suzie. His belief is tethered for he can give splendid reasons for his belief and, let us add, what makes his belief true – Suzie – figures in the causal explanation of his belief. Furthermore, he can easily distinguish Suzie from the other women staying at the seaside resort. It is appropriate for him to claim knowledge – and knowledge he has – or so it seems. Here come some problems.

Harry is now told that Suzie's twin sister has flown in and that she has been seen heading in his direction. He is also told that Suzie has been feeling unwell – the previous night had been rowdy – and so she has been thinking of remaining taverna-bound, nursing a hangover. Harry now wonders whether he had in fact seen Suzie. His belief that it was Suzie has broken loose from its tether. For all he can tell, maybe it was the twin sister. Yet, in fact, it was Suzie.

Suppose the information has not been presented to Harry; but consider another counterfactual: were Harry to receive that information, he would no longer be sure whom he saw. So, we may doubt whether Harry knows that Suzie walked by, even though he has not been presented with the sisterly evidence.

Were he to possess that evidence, it would undermine his reasons for his belief and any claims to knowledge. His justification is defeasible because of *evidence he does not possess*. We may align that thought to the earlier 'no false step' proposal: the reasoning by Harry, it may be argued, implicitly involves the false belief that the twin sister is not in the resort or that he knows the difference between Suzie and her twin – or between seagulls and eagles.

Harry's inability to distinguish between Suzie and twin in such circumstances, and between species of birds, establishes that he is not a reliable information source.

Sadly, more troubling complexities arise. Suppose the evidence is merely that Suzie has a twin sister, yet there is no reason whatever to believe that she is in town. Is the mere fact of a twin sister – or a look-alike somewhere in the universe – sufficient to show that Harry's belief is insufficiently well tethered? The problem is becoming that of determining which evidence and which possibilities are relevant for assessment of defeasibility and reliability. That a look-alike Suzie is in town, earlier thinking of sunbathing and then heading Harry's way, may seem highly relevant to whether Harry knows that Suzie walked by. That a look-alike Suzie exists somewhere in the universe is surely irrelevant. There is considerable greyness between those two extremes.

Suppose the information about Suzie's twin sister's presence in the resort is misinformation: Suzie has no sisters. If the misinformation is passed to Harry, he will lose his confident belief that he saw Suzie. His justification is as much defeasible by misinformation, it may seem, as by accurate. If true belief, to be knowledge, needs to be so stable, so strongly tethered to the believer's mind, to withstand all possible misinformation, then we should quickly collapse into deep scepticism. It is easy to dream up misleading outlandish information that, were it to be encountered, would lead us to drop virtually any belief.

# WITTGENSTEIN'S CHALLENGE: OUR USE OF 'KNOW'

It is easy to succumb to the thought that at least I know about many of my own psychological states: I know that I am in pain, that I have a tickling sensation, and what I am thinking. Knowledge of others' psychological states, though, is doubtful; I infer their psychological states from their behaviour. Wittgenstein, in controversial contrast, writes:

> In what sense are my sensations private? Well, only I can know whether I am really in pain; another person can only surmise it. – In one way this is wrong, and in another nonsense.
>
>   If we are using the word 'to know' as it is normally used (and how else are we to use it?), then other people very often know when I am in pain. – Yes, but all the same not with the certainty with which I know it myself! – It can't be said of me at all (except perhaps as a joke) that I know I am in pain. What is it supposed to mean – except perhaps that I am in pain?

The paragraph has given rise to many musings – for and against. One fertile thought is that it is mistaken to treat 'I am in pain' as descriptive. Rather, Wittgenstein suggests, it is akin to a sophisticated shriek or groan. If so, then to say 'I know, I am certain, that I am in pain' is like saying 'I know, I am certain' followed by a shriek or groan which is, indeed, a piece of grammatical nonsense.

  Another thought is the question, 'Where do we get the idea that knowledge must exclude even the possibility of error?' Wittgenstein writes:

> I can know what someone else is thinking, not what I am thinking.
> It is correct to say 'I know what you are thinking' and wrong to say 'I know what I am thinking.'
>   (A whole cloud of philosophy condensed into a drop of grammar.)

Perhaps the most valuable thought is that to understand our concept of knowledge, we need to reflect on how 'know' is normally used and for what purpose.

# Stepping back

The complexities above arise when trying to secure a grip on what more is needed such that true belief rises to knowledge – and, indeed, what is needed to justify people in their knowledge claims. The examples – there are numerous in the literature – may encourage us to challenge the assumption that knowledge is best understood by discovering its necessary and sufficient conditions. Perhaps that is a fool's quest. Perhaps we need to pay far more attention to circumstances and not look for a 'one-size fits all' solution – that craving for generality derided by Wittgenstein.

Dissatisfaction with the traditional analysis format has led a few philosophers to argue that the state of knowing is very different from that of believing. Now, if that difference resides solely in the relations that the two types of states have to other states, then that is nothing controversial. Beliefs sometimes transform into knowledge. Here is an analogy.

A man in Istanbul today is not a grandparent. Tomorrow because of what happens in London – namely, that his daughter gives birth – he is a grandparent. The man has undergone a change – known in the trade as a 'Cambridge change' – a change resting solely on things external to him having changed. So, too, arguably the sole difference between a Harry who knows that Suzie is on the beach and a Harry, otherwise identical, who does not know but believes that Suzie is on the beach, may just be that in the former case Suzie is on the beach, in the latter she is not.

♈

Beliefs come in degrees of strength – as do justifications. Furthermore, how strongly we are committed to a belief, and how strong a justification we require, depends on context: on the alternatives, on the urgency, on surrounding conversations. Such factors also arise with regard to whether we make a claim to know something. We may casually and readily claim to know that *p*, yet under certain challenges, certain persistence, we weaken. That concerns our *claims* to know; yet we should also be mindful – and here is a controversial suggestion – that whether our state is one of *knowing* that *p* also needs context qualifiers.

Let us focus on information acquisition – surely a key concern when interested in whether someone knows something. We seek information from within a context, one in which we already take for granted some background information, assume certain possibilities are ruled in, others out. We may want to know from Harry whether Suzie or some other woman from the taverna had walked by; the question of whether there are any Suzie twin sisters or look-alikes in town does not arise for us. So long as Harry can distinguish between Suzie and the other known tavern guests, he is a good informant. His giving us the truth is good enough for the context, for our purposes.

This chapter began with the traditional focus on 'knowing *that p*'; we are now touching on the importance of 'knowing *whether*' and 'knowing *how*'; indeed, 'knowing *how*' arose with the reliability feature.

If context is relevant, not merely regarding whether individuals are justified in claiming to know, but also regarding whether they do know, then that may explain, with philosophical thought experiments, why intuitions so often vary about whether someone knows or not. True, there is a thread common to all cases of propositional knowledge, namely that what is known needs to be true; but, that apart – well, circumstances dictate the demands made regarding the strength and type of tethering and belief.

When Harry can provide justifications for what he believes – and when his belief is strong – we have reasons to think that he is a good informative source. Even when Harry is uncertain, if we know that he is likely to be causally linked to the truth, able to discriminate sufficiently for our purposes, then what he tells us may constitute knowledge. We may ask *why* he believes or *how* it is that he knows, the different expressions pointing to different ways of manifesting being a good informant. The 'Why?' leads Harry into giving reasons, evidence, for his belief's truth. The 'How?' leads to his explaining the good position he may hold for true belief acquisition. The answers may, of course, coincide.

'Who went down to the beach earlier today?' we ask. Harry answers, 'Suzie.' We do not yet know whether Harry is a good informant. After all, he may have been guessing or relying on someone else; so, we ask whether he knows it was her. 'Yes, I'm sure it was Suzie,' answers Harry, his answer indicating certainty.

The answers may satisfy us, but we may need more; perhaps we were aiming to see Sandy. 'Sure it wasn't Sandy?' we ask. Harry replies, 'Certainly not – I know my Suzie from Sandy.'

That level of discrimination may satisfy us; yet if we add more to the context, dissatisfaction may come to the fore. Suppose we have been told of Suzie's twin sister arriving. What may now be relevant is whether Harry can visually distinguish between the twins. We press our worry onto him; he bats it away. 'No problem,' he says, 'that's all a mistake – she has no twin.' And so our worry may be quelled, or we may have more factors to bowl at him. Of course, we could spin some very outlandish possibilities – as sceptics would do – to see if every ground for doubt can be dismissed. 'If you *really* know, then you must be able to distinguish Suzie from Sandy, from a twin, from a possible twin, from a perfect impersonator' – and so forth.

Those sceptical 'really's are for the next chapter. For this chapter, we rest with the following thoughts.

In our ordinary use of knowledge and reliance on those who know, demands for discriminations, for deeper discernments, come to an end. Where that end is depends on the particular context, our practical needs, and the cases at hand. That context, those needs, the particularities of the everyday, may be absent from – or too readily overlooked when within – the philosophy seminar. Once bewildered by a concept, sense suggests that we should head home to the commonplace – wherein reside both the source and the value of our concepts.

We should have regard for a thought from the eighteenth-century Novalis, an author, poet and minor philosopher of early German romanticism; the thought is:

> Philosophy is properly home-sickness; the wish to be everywhere at home.

# 8

# How sceptical should we be?

Perfectly sensible and reasonable people – people who know that the Earth orbits the Sun, that a few days ago it rained, that next week there will still be fish in the sea – when within the philosophical seminar often undergo a remarkable change. Suddenly, they feel that they do not really know such matters – or so they say, and they say with seeming sincerity. They have become sceptics: they doubt the possibility of knowledge.

Scepticism can be traced to the ancient Greek Pyrrho of Elis. Some sceptics would claim that nothing can be known – not even that nothing can be known. Ancient anecdotes abound of Pyrrho ignoring precipices, dangerous dogs and other hazards for he had no good reason to trust his senses. Fortunately, he had good friends who were not so sceptical; they steered him away from disasters in waiting. The sceptical aim was for tranquillity, for life unperturbed by social conventions, unruffled by bad news or even appalling pain from falling over a cliff – well, apparently so. Now, it is open to question whether we can live the life of a sceptic – it would surely be a short life, at least for the friendless – but scepticism raises deep puzzlements concerning what justifies our most basic beliefs about, and actions within, the world.

We encountered, in Chapter One, Descartes' attempted global scepticism, doubting everything as far as he could via the supposed possibility of an evil genius. Descartes sought, once and for all, foundations for knowledge; others accept that we are bound to be engaged in continuing revision. Before focusing on global scepticism, let us consider some less global scepticisms.

People usually constrain their scepticisms to particular locations: you may be sceptical about the possibility of moral knowledge, yet not of knowledge of other minds. In centuries past, many doubted scientific 'knowledge', but not God's existence. Today we may be sceptical of economic theories and even the latest cosmological theory, yet rest content with much of science.

Bertrand Russell, the eminent twentieth-century logician, Nobel Prize winner and controversial campaigner – additionally distinguished by being thrown into prison twice, dismissed from his Cambridge college and from New York's City College, over a lifetime that spanned 97 years – noted that our present evidence is compatible with the universe having come into existence five minutes ago, carrying our apparent memories of a past, 'fossil records' and food being well beyond its use-by date. There is a gap between the present evidence and what the evidence is evidence for, a gap between the tomatoes' mould and the inferred fact that they were bought some time ago: the evidence *underdetermines* what it is evidence for. Once there is a gap, a logical gap, the sceptic strikes. Here, the sceptic casts doubt on our alleged knowledge of the past and may question the very existence of a past.

Curiously, people are typically more comfortable with accepting some knowledge of the past than of the future. Perhaps we can see into the past through memory. Because of light's travelling time, we perceive distant stars as they were millennia ago. Future events, though, do not yet exist – are not now. We may respond that past events, being past, also do not exist now. True, things may not turn out as predicted, but beliefs about the past can also be mistaken. Future discoveries affect not only whether we were right about the future, but whether we need to revise views about the past. For that matter, we can make mistakes about what is present to us right now.

Focusing on the future takes us into the local scepticism of inductive reasoning, brought to the fore by the, as ever, great David Hume.

## TWO MODELS FOR HANDLING SCEPTICISM

**Descartes** employed his method of systematic doubt, to uncover foundations for knowledge. Here is his famous 'apples' model:

> Suppose someone had a basket of apples and, being worried that some were rotten, wanted to take out the rotten ones to prevent the rot spreading. Would he not begin by tipping out the whole lot? Would not the next step be to cast his eye over each apple in turn, returning to the basket only those apples he saw to be sound?
>
> Now, those who have never philosophized correctly have various opinions derived from childhood, and which may in many cases be false. They need to separate the false beliefs from the others, to prevent the false ones from contaminating the rest and making the whole lot uncertain. The best way to accomplish this is to reject all their beliefs in one go, as if they were all uncertain and false. They can then go over each belief in turn and re-adopt only those which they recognize to be true and not open to doubt.

Matters are not as simple as the model suggests. We need to retain some beliefs as true, for example, those concerning sound reasoning, in order to evaluate which apples – which beliefs – ought to be discarded and which accepted.

**Otto Neurath**, of the twentieth century's Vienna Circle, with its emphasis on empirical observation for knowledge acquisition, proposed a more realistic model:

> We are like sailors who must rebuild their ships on the open sea, never able to dismantle them in dry-dock and to reconstruct them there out of the best materials.

We must accept some beliefs as true, in order to assess others. That does not rule out revisiting those accepted beliefs for assessment. There are, though, certain beliefs and argument forms – the reliance on consistency, on beliefs cohering – that must, it seems, be held firm, unless we are persuaded by Willard van Orman Quine, a distinguished recent American, distinguished both by his logical prowess and his name, who insisted, 'Everything is revisable.' Perhaps he should have added, 'except the claim that everything is revisable'.

# Not the black swan again: conjectures, refutations and science

Philosophers, even best-selling authors, cannot resist telling the old, old, tale of the black swan. Once, the available evidence for European zoologists pointed to all swans being white. From the evidence – let us pretend – of a million swans being white, they concluded, with high confidence, that all swans are white, the implication being that future swans sighted will be white. That is inductive reasoning by enumeration. One day, though, along comes a black swan or, more accurately, one day, in Australia, a black swan is sighted. The universal generalization, 'All swans are white', has been falsified, refuted, by evidence of a single black swan.

The universal swan generalization was offered as an empirical proposition, one that could be refuted – and it was refuted. Refutation, though, could have been resisted, at least for a while, despite the black plumage spied. The alleged truth of the generalization might have led to insistence that the creature with black feathers could not therefore have been a swan. The generalization's true status may then have been revealed as no longer an interesting substantial claim about the whitish ways of swan worlds, a claim discovered to be false. Instead, the generalization became but a stipulation about the meaning of the word 'swan', making 'all swans are white' true by definition.

Resistance to jettisoning empirical generalizations need not manifest such definitional insistence. There could have been freak lighting conditions, or proper examination may have shown the bird radically different from swans. One swallow does not make a summer (an aphorism from Aristotle) and one challenging observation to a universal generalization does not necessarily establish the generalization false. If, though, after further investigation, we find nothing odd about the lighting, nothing odd about the creature's internal constitution, then the swan generalization needs rejection.

The example started with inductive reasoning; the general inductive form is as follows:

Premiss:       All observed items that are *F* are *G*.
Conclusion:    All items that are *F* are *G*.

The '*F*' and '*G*' flag properties, such as being a swan and being white. Even if the premiss is true, the conclusion may not be true: the argument is not deductively valid. As explained in Chapter One, with a valid deduction, if the premisses are true, then it necessarily follows that the conclusion is true.

Inductive reasoning relies on nature having certain uniformities across the observed and the unobserved; but what can justify belief in such uniformities? There is sometimes the thought that if the inductive premiss covers numerous observed items, then it is at least likely that all items that are *F* are *G*. That thought merits challenge: knowledge of that likelihood would require knowing the total number of *F* items, observed and unobserved – even throughout the whole universe.

Scientific theories rely in some way on observations. The theories involve universal generalizations, expressions of so-called laws of nature assumed to apply across the universe, be they concerning forces, acceleration and mass, or relationships between pressures and volumes of gases, or boiling points of liquids and efficacy of antibiotics. The term 'theory', by the way, need convey no doubt or speculation. Reflect on the huge successes of numerous scientific theories and applications, from electrical equipment to medical treatments to transportation. How do we account for such seeming scientific knowledge, if induction lacks good justification?

Some – notably Karl Popper in the twentieth century – have vehemently argued that the scientific enterprise should not be understood as inductive, as collecting observations and inferring universal generalizations; rather, focus on 'conjectures and refutations'. Scientists do, or at least ought to, put forward bold empirical conjectures or hypotheses – all metals expand when heated; all swans are white – and then conduct investigations involving predictions. If the predictions turn out mistaken, then the investigated conjecture is refuted, falsified, and must be discarded, though a revised conjecture could subsequently be offered for testing. If the conjecture is not refuted, it should not be believed as true, but merely accepted as deserving further challenges. One day it may yet be refuted – this is scientific fallibilism – and many scientific theories, from the Ptolemaic to the Newtonian, have been refuted. Indeed, Popper's rejection of induction arguably has the paradoxical consequence that rationally we should have no greater confidence in a theory that has survived many tests than one that has been tested only a little and has survived.

As implied with the swan tale, a hypothesis does not confront the world alone. When some disturbing evidence is encountered, we may cling to the tested hypothesis and revise either auxiliary generalizations assumed true or our beliefs about the initial conditions. If a theory predicts that the new cosmetic developed will cause cell changes, then if the changes fail to materialize, maybe the theory was mistaken – but maybe the tested skin types were other than thought or the testing apparatus unreliable. Readers may recall physics lessons: if experiments failed to deliver expected results, the experiments (or experimenters) were assumed faulty, not that the relevant scientific theory had been falsified.

A crude refutational methodology needs itself, therefore, to be revised to recognize that rogue experimental results may be explained by factors other than the falsity of the generalization tested. Paradoxically, an unfalsifiable assumption, that no unknown factors affect the experiments, is required. Further – also paradoxically – it is accepted that a hypothesis's past failure to predict correctly is sufficient to deem it a failure for all future time.

Scientists, in fact, develop research programmes, judging which investigations may be fruitful; they operate within a paradigm – certain basic theories, a general world view – and that paradigm, it has been argued, may be jettisoned only when a revolutionary new perspective takes hold. The jettisoning happens when the old paradigm becomes too unwieldy, with too many auxiliary hypotheses and caveats introduced to protect it from counter-evidence – when the paradigm offends Ockham's Razor not to multiply entities beyond necessity. The classic, though controversial example, is the revolutionary shift from the Ptolemaic paradigm of the Earth as the universe's centre to the heliocentric, sun-centred view, with Copernicus claiming, 'Finally we shall place the Sun himself at the centre of the universe.'

Scientific developments partially depend on research programmes and those programmes depend on social factors, funding mechanisms, taboos and political correctness: funding may be unavailable, investigations halted – for example, because of protests against animal experimentation, lack of anticipated profitability, or political unease at investigations into sexual differences. Also, scientists sometimes simply move on: rogue results are forgotten, consigned to dusty volumes awaiting visits by dusty historians decades later. There remains, though, the basic true thought that theories, if making substantial claims about the world, are open to refutation and should be tested. That is science at its best for Popper: contrast with pseudo-science which protects itself from counter-evidence. Astrology is pseudo-scientific, it seems, for the predictions are typically so vague that whatever happens can be interpreted as in accord with them. Controversially, some argue that psychoanalysis and religious claims are pseudo-scientific: what possible evidence is allowed to count against them?

## Adam and Eve, bricks and glass – and habits

Is the ready dismissal of induction justified? We see a brick heading for the glass window. Surely we have good reason to believe that the glass will break; our reason is based on past breakage experiences. To misuse an example from Hume, consider an Adam and Eve in a Garden of Eden, curiously a garden with glass windows and bricks. On the first tantrum occasion of Adam throwing a brick at a glass window (closed), they may have no expectations regarding consequences; but once glass smashes have been experienced, they expect similar results when bricks again hit glass. They have habits, expectations.

The correct analysis of causation is controversial, but, as earlier suggested, if C causes E, then had C not occurred, E would not have occurred. That counterfactual analysis – 'counterfactual' indicating what would have happened counter to what in fact happened – requires nuancing. Still, experiences of C-type events followed by E-type events, and of E-type events not occurring in the absence of C-type events, may suggest that particular C-type events cause particular E-type events. Hume further suggested that the mind possesses a propensity to spread itself onto the world: the expectations that have arisen from experience are misunderstood as worldly metaphysical glue – mentioned earlier in Chapter Two – sticking effects to causes: the glass *must* break under the flying brick; the water *must* boil when heated. That Humean explanation cannot do as it stands because the mind's propensity to spread itself onto the world itself involves causality – and so cannot be part of the understanding of causality without danger of circularity, possibly vitiating the understanding.

Our understanding of physical objects includes their interaction with other objects. Glass to be glass (unreinforced) is such that it breaks under flying brick impact. That leads to a mythical means of justifying induction. If we see bricks hitting glass panes, we know that the panes will break – otherwise, they would not have been glass. Yet that thought simply moves the inductive problem elsewhere for, until the pane breaks, we cannot be sure that it is glass. It is no use examining the pane's molecular structure to establish what will happen, for we then encounter the inductive puzzle of how that structure will behave this time round.

Induction may be salvaged, some suggest, by transforming it into a deduction with an additional premiss, one needing considerable care:

Premiss 1:    In diverse contexts, all observed items that are F are G.

Premiss 2:    All regularities observed in diverse contexts continue when unobserved.

Conclusion:  All items that are F are G.

Care is required because Premiss 2's implied uniformity raises questions of degree. After all, the white swans were observed in many different European contexts. That I continue to breathe day after day does not indicate that I breathe day after every day. Whatever caveats we may reasonably press upon the uniformity premiss, we may ask what justifies holding the premiss true. It is no self-evident truth. We can reach it neither by *a priori* argument in the way of mathematics, nor justly support it, without circularity, through our experiences. Doubtless there are evolutionary explanations of why induction-loving creatures are alive and well or relatively well; but that merely shows inductive reasoning's *past* success. A radical approach links God to the reliability of inductive reasoning, yet that magnifies problems, those problems of God's nature and ways divine, ways often deemed 'mysterious'.

Maybe we should simply accept that we have unjustifiable inductive habits and cannot escape. That is Hume's naturalistic – though somewhat defeatist – approach.

# The scandal

A scandal exists in philosophy – so announced Kant – though a scandal far removed from exposures of the tabloid press.

The scandal is the absence of proof for the very existence of things outside us; that is, of independently existing objects in time and space, independent of our experiences. Recall Chapter One's evil genius, the experience machine and the dreaming possibility. To have knowledge beyond me, as already said, requires a leap across the epistemological gap – a gap between my evidence and what the evidence is evidence for.

Consider a sceptical argument where '$p$' may be replaced by a vast number of propositions typically accepted as known:

Premiss 1:    If you know that $p$, then you know that you cannot be mistaken that $p$.

Premiss 2:    You do not know that you cannot be mistaken that $p$.

Conclusion:  You do not know that $p$.

The argument is deductively valid. Are its premisses true? Well, Premiss 2 appears true because you may be dreaming, you may be misinformed or Descartes' evil genius may be at work. Premiss 1 relies on knowledge's curiously named 'closure principle', roughly thus: if you know that $p$ and you know that $p$ entails $q$, then you know that $q$. Now, as you know that $p$, you may feel that it must surely follow that you *are not* mistaken that $p$ and you know that to be so; but, as seen in the previous chapter, it does not follow that you need to know that you *cannot* be mistaken. The sceptic, though, may push on, insisting that you only know that you are not mistaken if you can show how you have leapt the logical gap such that you indeed cannot be mistaken – and that gap you cannot leap.

Once we gaze at the gap – the gap between evidence and what the evidence is for – we may reason that it must be illusory: there can exist nothing on the other side of the evidence. The gap is pure emptiness. All that I have to go on are my own experiences, so how can I judge what, if anything, is beyond them? The sceptical conclusion may be stronger than that question hints.

Perhaps I cannot even conceive or make sense of things existing non-experienced – more sceptically, of things non-experienced *by me* – more sceptically still, of things non-experienced *by me now*? Such moves collapse us into extreme solipsism according to which I alone exist; well, only I and my experiences. The world reduces to me or, to see it differently, I am enlarged to envelop the whole world.

Physical objects – fast foods and feathers, watermelons and wheelbarrows – have sometimes been understood as mind-dependent entities, as being collections of experiences of colours, shapes and so forth – argued for by Bishop Berkeley. To overcome the counterintuitive thought that, therefore, such items do not exist when I fail to undergo the relevant experiences, Berkeley wheels in God: collections of ideas exist in, are dependent upon, God. Further, courtesy of God, I have reasons to believe that there are other finite spirits or minds. Berkeley's dictum, as seen, is 'to be is to be perceived' – and here is the additional, but oft forgotten – 'or to perceive'. Existence hangs on either perceiving or being immediate objects of perception.

A nuanced line, in the spirit (!) of Berkeley, is phenomenalism: physical objects are constructions from experiences and counterfactual truths concerning experiences that would occur were certain perceiving circumstances to obtain. Apart from formidable difficulties in specifying such circumstances solely by means of experiences and counterfactuals, phenomenalism traps the individual perceiver – the *I, me* – within a circle of ideas, without good reason to believe that others exist. A scandal remains unresolved.

G. E. Moore offered common sense for disposing of Kant's scandal. The disposal, a 1939 British Academy lecture, was aptly, though not modestly, entitled 'Proof of an External World'. Was there a highly technical argument? There was not. The proof, in essence, consisted of Moore saying and doing the following:

I can prove now, for instance, that two human hands exist. How?
By holding up my two hands, and saying, as I make a certain

gesture with the right hand, 'Here is one hand', and adding, as I make a certain gesture with the left, 'and here is another'.

By acting thus, Moore claimed to prove the existence of external things. His proof constitutes a proof, Moore insists, because the premises differ from the conclusion, the conclusion follows from the premises and Moore knows the premises to be true. The common response is that the proof misses the point, misses the gap. Moore has visual sensations *as if* of a hand, but he may be mistaken; so, he cannot know that there is a hand.

Moore's approach should not be so readily dismissed. First, it may bring home the clash between common sense and the sceptical stance. Do we really not know that we have bodies, that we live in a world with trees, treacle and thunderstorms – and with other people? The clash is stunning. Look around and try to interpret all as mere experiences within you. Can you really do so? Secondly, are we truly more certain that the sceptics' arguments are sound than that there is an external world, that we have genuine memories and are right to use induction? Are we truly more certain of the closure principle mentioned above than that we know that we have limbs, live on Earth and sometimes get tipsy from champagne?

# The mesh – or the babbling sceptic

Some distinguish between internal and external questions. Internally, within the mesh or framework of the acceptance of physical objects, we can assess whether we have good or bad grounds for what we say. The man tipsy from excess whisky is unreliable when counting hands; the sober philosophy professor is a better judge. Moore reminds us of that – and his practice also reminds us of fallibility. Once, when lecturing in an unfamiliar theatre, he looked up, declaring that he knew there to be a skylight above. He was later informed that it was just the ceiling painted that way. 'How ought I to have responded?' worried Moore in his notebooks.

The sceptical 'external' question – one asked by those philosophically sober, or tipsy? – becomes: what justifies acceptance of the overall framework, of external objects, of a past, of good methods of reasoning? An answer often given, as seen with induction, is naturalism. Naturalism is, though, no justification, but more a shrug of resignation with intimations of justificatory irrelevance: our biological nature determines not only that we must breathe, but also that we must judge and reason in certain ways. That is an end of the matter.

That reference to reason needs reflection. Extreme sceptics insist that there is a gap between what strikes us as good argument and what the reality is, if indeed any such reality exists. Protagoras insisted that 'man is the measure of all things': all truth is relative to the believer. Asserting that *p* is true is asserting merely that *p* is true *for you*. That latter could benignly mean merely that you believe *p* to be true – an objective truth about what you believe – but, it seems, Protagoras intended to convey the absence of objective truth, an idea met earlier, but then restricted to morality, challenging the objectivity of moral truth.

Suppose we engage Protagoras in discussion about his position. Such discussion presupposes objective truths: for example, that we are in discussion and whether his relativism is itself just relative. Indeed, that latter question casts doubt on the coherence of extreme scepticism. Here is how.

*Modus ponens* – a common term in philosophy – is an everyday argument form: If *p*, then *q*; *p*: therefore *q*. If Evelyne went to the party, people would have had a merry time; she did go to the party: therefore, people did have a merry time. To question whether such reasoning is good would be a sign of madness. Madness was, in fact, a hypothesis in Descartes' method of doubt, swiftly discarded presumably because we must deploy reasoning powers when assessing scepticism.

The quick answer to sceptics of *all* truth and reasoning is that, if there are no objective facts, their position is self-contradictory: they claim good reasons for thinking that there can be no good reasons. To raise sceptical doubts, we must use language, grasp concepts and recognize good reasoning. The best a global sceptic – one whose doubts extend to reason and objective truths – can do is babble meaninglessly – and babble without good reason. Those comments do not imply that we need never check our reasoning in particular cases. They do not even imply that there are no paradoxical contexts where even *modus ponens*, for example, may need handling with nuances.

To swim we need water; to reason we need logic. We need also the mesh of inductive practices and acceptance of mind-independent physical objects. Moore claimed to know a motley mash of basic empirical propositions, propositions such as: the Earth has existed for many, many years past; many human beings have been born; numerous physical objects exist independently of human beings. Now, if – *if* – doubt concerning such claims is impossible, then some argue – notably Wittgenstein – that paradoxically we lack knowledge of those claims. The framework of such 'hinge' propositions forms scaffolding rather than foundations. The scaffolding, the mesh, sets the arena within which knowledge and doubt are possible.

Consider the proposition that physical objects exist independently of human beings. We do not reason to it as the best or simplest explanation of our experiences. Indeed, it is far from simple. Reflect how scientific investigations lead to suggestions of unobserved subatomic entities: do such entities really exist or should we adopt 'instrumentalism', understanding them as theoretical constructs or tools that aid predictive powers? Reflect too how scientific investigations suggest that some qualities, 'secondary qualities' in Locke's terms – for example, colours – do not

# WHAT THE TORTOISE SAID TO ACHILLES

**Lewis Carroll,** of *Alice in Wonderland* fame, tells of Achilles the ancient Greek runner, now impressed by deductive logic. He shows off to the sceptical tortoise (who won a race against him) by showing the tortoise the power of logic. Consider a *modus ponens*:

Premiss 1:    If Socrates is a man, then Socrates is mortal.
Premiss 2:    Socrates is a man.
Conclusion:  Socrates is mortal.

The tortoise scratches his shell, unsure whether he should accept the conclusion. 'Look,' insists Achilles, 'you must surely see that if those two premisses are true then it must follow that the conclusion is true. 'Ah,' replies the tortoise, 'that sounds like another premiss. Please write it down; maybe I can then accept your argument.' So, Achilles inserts in the above argument:

Premiss 3: If Premisses 1 and 2 are true, then the conclusion is true.

'Mr Tortoise,' declares Achilles triumphantly, 'you must now accept the conclusion, for otherwise logic will grab you by the throat.' Yet the tortoise remains unmoved and sceptical, save for more scratching, now of head. 'I still don't quite see how you reach the conclusion.'

'Look,' replies Achilles, tetchily, 'if those three premisses hold, then it follows that the conclusion holds.' To that, the tortoise smiles, pointing out that Achilles has declared another 'if, then' premiss; that too needs to be written down as Premiss 4. Even Achilles now fumblingly sees how things are going; he is on a never-ending task.

**The moral**: if we try to justify *modus ponens* or any basic valid deduction by further premisses, we reach no end. Sometimes deductions are justified by rules, yet that raises similar problems – of introducing rules to justify rules. Valid forms are derived from particular cases of valid reasoning, needing no further justification. True, in long deductions, in arithmetical calculations, we may check our work by repeating the reasoning: that is, we resort to inductive practices. Such practices, though, are not justifying the reasoning's validity.

The lack of justification for valid deductions indicates defects neither in human logical insight nor in the deductions. We need often to resist sceptics' demands for further justifications. Explanations have to come to an end – and so do justifications.

exist 'out there' akin to our experiences, but are powers residing within objects, powers that cause us certain experiences. To get such speculations and investigations going – and some degree of scepticism – we need the scaffolding.

Care is required. In Moore and Wittgenstein's day, they would speak of the impossibility of men having been on the moon – a part of the scaffolding. Today, ignoring the example's past tense, the example provokes giggles. We need to be open to the possibility of hinge propositions being revised. Another of Wittgenstein's metaphors refers to a river's bank; it consists partly of hard rock open to no alteration and partly of sand which gets washed away and replaced.

Consider the apparent possibility of global deception cour-tesy of Descartes' evil genius. Can we make sense of that decep-tion? Arguably, we cannot. The evil genius's deception would be so good that the world would carry on as we should normally expect. Suppose the world is really made of treacle, but the genius deceives us into thinking otherwise, into thinking that televisions and trees, onions and washing machines are made from different material. We think that nothing is made of treacle, well, except treacle. If there is no way of grasping how it could be all treacle, no possible way of testing, of verifying or refuting, well, we may doubt the content of the deception. The genius is too clever and not just by half. The deception goes up in a puff of smoke.

Propositions that form the hard rock of the river's bank cannot be verified or refuted, yet are essential for us to make any sense at all, even to put forward the evil genius's deception. I must accept, for example, that entities other than me exist; that there is a distinction between appearance and reality; that I grasp the meanings of words. That still, of course, leaves plenty of room for doubt, for mistakes, for revisions.

Problems persist in making sense of a framework – a river's bank, scaffolding, or mesh – which itself is necessary for sense.

Perhaps to ask whether a 'hard rock' proposition is true – a proposition such as, there are mind-independent physical objects – is as senseless as asking whether the chessboard itself made a good move. Moves in chess can be evaluated as good or bad for winning the game; but the chessboard cannot be assessed as a good or bad move. The assessment of the chessboard is patent nonsense. None the less, questioning the existence of physical objects, of an external world, may still fascinate and may appear far from nonsense.

Appearances can be misleading.

## The stars, meaning and private languages

Look at the stars in the sky. 'There's Cassiopeia; here's Orion's Belt – see, over yonder, the Plough.' Did constellations exist before humans existed?

Constellations depend on patterns and resemblances that strike us. We have carved up the heavens; we could have grouped the stars differently. Once we muse thus, it is difficult to stop. The world, we may conclude, does not come to us ready carved as pebbles and ponds, mountains and monsoons, stars and seas. Those carvings rest on our concepts, concepts determined by our nature, by our being mobile 'biological blobs' with needs and interests. Kant spoke of 'things in themselves' – the noumena – which necessarily elude us; indeed, we are not justified in even applying the plural or singular to what is beyond all grasp. Mind you, if we seek to step outside our concepts, it hardly surprises that we lack all conception.

The picture that generates the problem here is that of humans separated from the world. Were the picture correct, I should reflect on my concept of human being. That too would be the result of my carving – as would be the conceptual distinction

I draw between others and myself. Deep and dark metaphysical disquiet haunts us; possibly the pathway to light is to resist the lure of 'I *versus* the world'. Let us blink in that light.

My concepts are not intrinsically mine, but shared. Further, those concepts do not arise while we humans sit back, contemplating the world, but by active engagement (indeed, sitting is already a biological engagement). We breathe – eat, drink and pass out waste. We trip and grab, hammer and saw, changing the world – changing ourselves. We bleed and bond, embrace and dismiss. Without that engagement, we should lack numerous concepts – and arguably should lack the groundings for abstract concepts, even the mathematical. We did some similar doubt-casting in Chapter Six, when considering computers and robots.

Worthy of mention here is Wittgenstein's famous yet controversial rejection of the possibility of a private language. A private language, in the philosophers' sense, is one concerning which *only* I can possibly know the meanings of my words. We are lured by the picture of our pains – aches, tingles and thoughts – being private to ourselves. I may conclude that no one else can know what my pains are like; no one else can even know what I mean by the word 'pain'. To correct that teasing picture, reflect how astonishing it is, then, that we speak a common language with words such as 'pains', 'aches' and 'tingles' – and that we rush to help screaming victims, not wondering what inferences to make from the screams. Reflect, too, on how you learnt 'sensation' words: parents, teachers, friends must have introduced them to you when they could tell, it seems, that you were hurting, imagining, itching and tingling.

A general sceptical puzzle arises here – some see as deep, others as nonsense – of language and meaning. In this introduction, we can present but a flavour, to encourage readers to explore. The puzzle was highlighted by the somewhat eccentric American logician Saul Kripke, controversially claimed by him as present in Wittgenstein's work. The scepticism again relies on a gap.

The common-sense belief is that usually I know what I mean when I use a word. What is it, though, that constitutes my meaning one thing rather than another? What makes it the case that my use of words in the future is the same as before (when it is)? The 'meaning sceptic' finds no acceptable answers.

Suppose we have been teaching a child the even numbers, 2, 4, 6, 8 … *and so on*. Suppose the child has successfully continued the series to a hundred. He has grasped what is meant by 'add two', we think. Yet has he? When instructed to carry on 'in the same way', he goes haywire. Perhaps he continues after a hundred with '2, 4, 6, 8' again; perhaps he goes '101, 103, 105', perhaps even '56, 98, 202'. What he considers as 'in the same way' differs from our consideration. We may run through millions of examples, yet they do not tell us what grasp he has of the meaning that fixes his future use as, in his terms, 'the same'. The evidence under-determines what he means. The scepticism extends: what fixes what we ourselves mean when we speak of continuing 'in the same way'? How do we know how we shall act 'in the same way' tomorrow?

A related puzzle is one version of Nelson Goodman's 'new riddle of induction'. Given the evidence, we expect future observed emeralds to be green, that is, to remain the 'same' colour. Suppose future emeralds observed, after say 31st December 2019, were blue: we would see them as changed in colour. Yet others – another community – may see them as remaining the same colour: their colour concept may have been 'grue', that is, what we understand as meaning: green until the 2019 date, then blue. They understand emeralds, in the circumstances supposed, both before and after the date mentioned as remaining the same colour, namely grue. Maybe all along they believed emeralds to be grue and predicted they would remain the same colour, namely grue - that is, being blue once into the 2020s.

The general problem is: how can we ever determine, even of ourselves, what constitutes 'going on in the same way'. The history of our use of a term does not fix what we mean to do in the future: there is a gap between use to date and future use. Wittgenstein suggests that we feel that there should be rails stretching out into future uses, to keep us on the straight and narrow; but there are no such rails.

Arguably, the mistake is for philosophers to demand more than can possibly be given. Here, the demand regarding what we mean is for something more than our natural recognition of continuing the same, of 'and so on' or, more minimally, for something more than our grasp of things continuing the same '...'.

Seeking something further to justify our grasp of the '...' is the mistake. We need to recognize when to use the full stop. Explanations must come to an end; and here is the full stop.

# 9

# God: for and against

When a rabbit is pulled from the magician's hat – a hat shown moments earlier to be empty – you wonder from whence came the creature, not that it came from nowhere. And when the lady is sawn in half before your very eyes, yet is miraculously later restored as whole, you think that is no miracle at all. Such conjuring tricks we take in our stride convinced that there are explanations, even when to us unknown. Yet turn to the universe as a whole and bafflement sets in, well, sets in for many. The universe popped into existence, some insist, yet from no hat and with no magician in view. Hence, it popped from nowhere and from nothing at all; to which others reply that existence from nothing, *ex nihilo*, is simply impossible.

So it is that we have the classic metaphysical debate: was the universe caused by something else and, if so, what is that else? The debate also provides a look-in for cosmologists, much exercised by the Big Bang tale and the resultant universe that supports life and consciousness – well, to some extent.

The universe, the world, in one understanding, embraces all that there is – but that would include God, if God exists. So, we need here to think of the universe, the world, as including all that there is without God; then we may see whether this universe points to a deity's existence.

God is standardly taken to possess certain attributes, ones more so than just (just?) being creator of this universe. Further, many believers in God, or indeed gods, do not recognize their belief as grounded solely in evidence or reason, but in faith. In this chapter, though, we look at the major philosophical arguments for God's existence, as a transcendent being, arguments to which many religious believers often defer.

The monotheistic God – of Judaism, Christianity and Islam – is typically understood as a being that is not merely one, but is all powerful, all knowing and all good. Those features are the well-known 'omni's – omnipotent, omniscient and omnibenevolent – though other features are often ascribed, for example, 'omnipresent' and being revealed through certain scriptures. For the sake of tradition and avoiding linguistic jarring, we use the traditional 'he' for God. Let us note, by the by, that some religions make scant mention of God or gods and even explicit monotheistic believers sometimes accept that their divine talk needs careful interpretation; the talk perhaps should not even suggest commitment to a transcendent being, but is rather a way of showing piety, respecting the world and mankind as a precious gift.

Usually, to establish that something exists, we turn to experience, to empirical research. Thus it is that we have *a posteriori* arguments for the divine existence, arguments that rely on some facts discovered through our worldly experiences. (Later on, we shall assess a key *a priori* argument, one that relies on reason alone.)

Two overwhelming facts about the universe are that it exists and that it possesses a certain orderly character. That it exists, it is often insisted, requires explanation: thus it is that the Cosmological Argument is presented, though sometimes that slides into distinct arguments concerning the world's contingency – that it just happens to be as it is – and that it allegedly has a beginning. That the world displays certain orderliness or seems finely tuned to life leads to various design arguments. And a seeming feature of our lives, namely objective morality, leads to moral arguments for God as divine lawgiver. It is to the main *a posteriori* arguments that we first turn – and we need to remember to restrict the arguments to their station. Even if, for example, we prove the existence of a divine designer, we have not thereby shown that that designer cares for humanity.

# The universe – botched?

Classic design arguments relied on the astonishing fact that parts of the body can function harmoniously for survival (well, for a few decades), that the environment and different species are interdependent and that, indeed, the universe is orderly, even manifesting beauty, under fixed laws of nature. Now, of course, evolutionary theory offers explanations of how eyes, ears and the like have developed and how species and environment interrelate. Further, we may let fly sceptical arrows at the universe's orderliness and beauty, when noticing the chaotic effects of earthquakes, tsunamis and cancers on the lives of millions, or when under the uncertain spell of quantum theory's claims of indeterminacy.

Whatever caveats the reflections above generate, we live in a universe with law-like regularities which commands certain feelings of awe and wonder. All that demands explanation – well, apparently so – and that is popularly expressed as: science tells us *how*, but not *why*, things are. That is straightaway misleading: science frequently answers 'why?' questions – why the apples fell; why the planets move as they do – but the explanations these days are causal not teleological, not of apples and planets having goals or purposes or a *telos* or end in view. We still often explain human actions in teleological terms – Why is she running? To catch the post – but many argue that even those are reducible to causal explanations: her desire to catch the post caused her running and that desire is a matter of certain neurological states.

William Paley, of the eighteenth century, read a few decades later by Charles Darwin, famously spoke of encountering a watch on a heath (later writers moved the watch from heath to seashore). Noticing the chronometer's harmonious internal workings, reason compels us to believe the item had been designed; such functional complexity would be incredible if from chance. Paley recognized that we could imagine watches reproducing themselves; yet we should still suppose a designer for the whole ticking array. By analogy with human contrivances, the remarkable workings of the universe, the creation of life, even by evolution, overwhelmingly suggest that the universe is designed and hence in need of a designer. That is, the universe requires a teleological explanation, an explanation in terms of a supernatural being's purposes. The usual assumption is that the divine designer is also creator of the stuff of the universe.

Now, the success of arguments resting on analogy depends upon the analogy's strength. The analogy here would need (dare we say) fine tuning. On the one hand, if we maintain a strong analogy holds, then the argument is deservedly exposed to David Hume's jibes for, as Hume points out, many human contrivances are the result of committees and apprentices, with changing plans and designs. Maybe this universe is but the first botched job of an infant deity. Indeed, we have no idea of divine purposes and hence no idea how well this universe meets any design. On the other hand, if we claim that the analogy is only weak, then the argument's force is indeed so much weakened.

One recent 'intelligent design' argument is that life involves an irreducible complexity which evolutionary theory cannot explain; evolutionists typically dismiss that. A bigger-scaled 'intelligent design' argument rests on the apparent fine tuning of the universe for life: had certain key physical constants been just a teeny bit different, then life would have been impossible. Now, what counts as life and its significance is moot, but presumably we are meant to be surprised at the existence of consciousness, reasoning and desire, if resulting from chance. An immediate thought is, if human life is so valuable – 'life' as shorthand for conscious rational creatures – and points to intelligent design, it is curious that there is so little life around, at least locally. Of course, it is possible that less is more – more valuable – where life, in contrast to a deity's power, is concerned.

Intelligent design as fine-tuning – we may controversially suggest – appears to manifest a conceit by its proposers for, even ignoring the assumption that consciousness is very valuable, their conviction is that they know what is necessary for the generation of conscious life. Beware those scientists who confidently believe that consciousness can arise *solely* from certain carbon-based life-forms. Let us clarify.

Philosophical fish swimming in a pond may rightly reason that the pond is sufficient for their swim, but ought not to conclude that ponds are necessary for their swimming – perhaps they could equally happily swim in rivers or lakes – for all that is necessary, given their existence, is a decent volume of decent water, be it river, lake or pond. That draws attention to a benign and obvious anthropic (or piscine) principle, namely that any natural laws – or ponds – observed are compatible with the existence of the observers, be they human or piscine. Whatever those conditions, whatever those laws – whatever the ponds – the benign anthropic principle neither explains why they exist nor shows which ones, if any of them, are necessary for human or piscine life.

The universe, it seems, could have been so very different in an infinite number of ways that, even if there are many unknown ways in which life could have arisen, the number of ways that rule out life may still be infinitely more numerous. Hence, we may continue to be surprised that the universe is one such that we exist, if its existence happened by chance. Let us muse further.

We should be astonished if, after random shuffles, a pack of cards turns out to be in suit and numerical order. That is incredibly unlikely, but it strikes us as so because we are familiar with that ordering. After all, any ordering, after random shuffling, is as unlikely as any other. Many remain amazed, though, that the existent universe is one that supports life. Indeed, *strong* anthropic principles are proposed, for example that only very specific features of a universe could generate life – even that the universe just is finely tuned, that is, designed for conscious life.

Consider any other universe that could have existed – from the pretended viewpoint of items within that universe. Suppose the universe consisted solely of pebbles, amoeba or entities unknown, of chaos or of bland homogeneity: how amazing, it may appear, that that universe existed with such features – yet features indicative of design? Such thoughts do not harmonize well with the fine-tuning argument for that argument relies on the perceived special features of this universe that generate human life. Proponents of the argument would be unimpressed with the intelligence in design, it seems, if the universe were such that any designer must have been Pollock-inspired, creating chaos, or Malevich-inspired, designing homogeneity.

Fine-tuning arguments assume that this universe's existence must be by chance if not explained by divine designing purposes. Now, probability is often understood in terms of the frequency of types of event happening – think of the expected frequency of the six turning up with dice throws – but the existence of the universe is a one-off; and we lack conceptual grip on the probability of a one-off. A reply grounds probability in terms of how likely it would or would not be for a divine designer to choose to create this world out of an infinite number of possible worlds, but then we could hardly use the improbability of this world to argue for a designer's existence: his existence has been presupposed in making sense of the probability.

## The universe – caused?

Whatever our feelings about alleged design, the simple fact that something should exist uncaused may engender surprise. In our everyday meanderings we meet no uncaused happenings. More accurately, we *assume* that there must be causes of happenings; and, it seems, the universe around us has happened. Now, some may crudely argue that every event must have a cause and that

## TYPING MONKEYS – AND GOD

God is often described as an infinite, all-powerful, all-knowing, all-good being. The infinite, though, is not an easy concept.

# The monkeys

Some cosmologists and mathematicians assert that, given infinite space or time, everything that could happen will happen and, indeed, must happen. The assertion is made vivid by proposing that, with infinite time, typing monkeys at some point must type the complete *oeuvre* of Shakespeare. That is a logical howler, if 'infinite' is used with its normal meaning of 'endless'. It howls because it is logically possible that monkeys type forever, endlessly, infinitely, yet the Shakespearean works remain untyped. However long the run, it is logically possible that your choice of lottery numbers never wins. Remember, logical possibility is just that which involves no contradiction.

Here is a related thought: the number of even numbers is infinite: 2, 4, 6, 8… goes on without end, yet it does not include all the numbers. That infinite, endless, series does not include the odd numbers. A question, indeed, is whether God's knowledge could embrace such endlessness.

# The multiverse

Those impressed by this universe's life-supporting features – surprising, if by chance – sometimes turn to explanations other than the divine. Certain cosmologists argue that our universe is but one of an infinite number, the total multitude being a multiverse, 'universe' (singular) no longer meaning everything open to physics. Universes composing the multiverse differ in their underlying constants and laws. So, if we accept that such different universes exist, it is no longer surprising that one of them – ours – supports life.

The multiverse line smacks of an *ad hoc* proposal driven by anti-divine desperation, yet at least it deploys concepts familiar to physicists – the different universes result from the familiar forces yet with different magnitudes – rather than divine mystery. Even if an infinite number of universes exist, that does not explain how this 'finely-tuned' one comes about. Even if all possible universes that can co-exist do exist, that does not explain this one's existence.

the series of causes and effects cannot go back infinitely, so therefore there must be a first cause – God's action – of all the events. That involves contradiction because a first cause has, of course, no cause. If every event has a cause, then we should expect there to be a cause of God's actions and so forth.

By definition, every *effect* has a cause, but we have no reason to think that every *event* is an effect. A coincidence may be considered an event, but there may be no cause of the coincidence, just causes of the events that coincide. Suppose everybody at a concert wears purple socks. What a coincidence! Well, it may be no coincidence at all, for perhaps the individuals were members of the purple sock party on its annual outing. Yet, it may be a sheer uncaused coincidence: the individuals were unconnected, but each chose purple socks that day.

Cosmological arguments are usually more subtle than the crude version above. One such argument is the Arabic Kalam; it takes as self-evident: everything with a beginning must have a cause. The argument gains current comfort from cosmologists' support for the universe exploding into existence about fourteen billion years ago. Now, cosmological theories are often revised; certainly we should not infer that evidence for the Big Bang rules out evidence for prior events. Many of us may contentedly accept that whenever past events are mentioned, we can make sense of the existence of prior causes: the event sequence could go back in time without end, infinitely so.

Suppose that sense can be made of the universe beginning. Ought we to conclude that it must have been divinely caused? Well, 'cause', as standardly understood, is a temporal concept, so we may question the sense of God's causing the universe's beginning including the beginning of time. Indeed, there can be no causal explanation of time's coming into existence, not least because there is no sense in the idea of time beginning.

That last thought may lead us to a more nuanced argument, one much promoted by Leibniz, namely the Argument from

Contingency. Items and events around us are all contingent, that is, they might not have been. Your existence is contingent on that of your parents' and theirs on their parents' – and we may trace back to earlier life forms and earlier still. Maybe the series of contingent items goes back in time without end just as maybe it goes forward in time without end.

Leibniz is content to accept such possible infinite series. He is, though, the supreme rationalist: he insists that there must be a reason or cause for everything. That is his Principle of Sufficient Reason, the apex of rationality. The universe might not have existed and might not have existed in the way that it does. Leibniz concludes that the universe, being thus contingent, even if with contingent items infinite in number, must be 'grounded in' something, explained by something, that is not itself contingent – that points to God, God understood as a necessary being, a being that by its very nature must exist, dependent on nothing else.

In opposition to Leibniz, it looks as if a necessary being cannot possibly be a sufficient explanation for any contingency. The universe, being contingent, might have been different. God, being a necessary existent, would also have existed with such a differently constructed universe. Therefore, anything necessary about him cannot be sufficient to explain the universe as it happens to be. So, a sufficient explanation would need at least reference to some divine contingent features – God's 'free' decisions, for example – but then the Principle of Sufficient Reason would set us searching for sufficient explanations for those contingencies of free decisions; that is, arguably a quest without end.

Perhaps we should accept either that it is a brute contingent fact that the universe exists as it does without explanation, or that the universe necessarily exists as it does, maybe flowing from a necessary divine being. That leads us, honouring an earlier promise, to look at the key *a priori* argument for God's existence – the

Ontological Argument (from the Greek *ont*, being) – an argument perhaps better seen as for God's necessary existence. The argument is most associated with the eleventh-century St Anselm, though later versions are defended by Descartes, Spinoza and Leibniz, and certain contemporary philosophers. Earlier versions lurk in some Ancient Greek thinking.

## The tobacco pouch

Bertrand Russell was once fascinated by the Ontological Argument. When walking along Trinity Lane Cambridge, he became convinced of its soundness – and with that he threw his tobacco pouch into the air with excitement. True, a few days later, the tobacco pouch came crashing down: he spotted the argument's errors, as he thought, and returned to his atheism.

Now, the presence of ideas or concepts of items does not standardly show that the items exist. We possess concepts of Santa Claus, unicorns and mermaids – that is, we know what they are – but from mere concept possession, it follows not at all that Santa Claus, unicorns and mermaids exist. We have the idea of the Loch Ness Monster, yet empirical research is required to discover whether there is such a monster, not abstract reasoning in philosophers' armchairs. The Ontological Argument insists that things are different with regard to God: by pure reason alone, his existence, it is claimed, can be known.

Here is the argument. The fool, by the way, is the atheist who understands what we mean by 'God', namely that being than which nothing greater can be conceived, yet believes that God does not exist.

Even the fool is convinced that something exists in the understanding, at least, than which nothing greater can be conceived. For, when he hears this, he understands it. And whatever is understood, exists in the understanding. And assuredly that, than which nothing greater can be conceived, cannot exist in the understanding alone. For, suppose it exists in the understanding alone: then it can be conceived to exist in reality, which is greater. Therefore, if that, than which nothing greater can be conceived, exists in the understanding alone, the very being, than which nothing greater can be conceived, is one, than which a greater can be conceived. But obviously, this is impossible. Hence, there is no doubt that there exists a being, than which nothing greater can be conceived, and it exists both in the understanding and in reality.

Anselm, using the atheist's premiss that the greatest being exists in the understanding but not in reality – that is, that there is no God – reaches the contradiction that it is conceivable that there be something greater than the greatest conceivable being. That is reduction to an absurdity: *reductio ad absurdum*. Hence, Anselm further concludes, assuming the other premisses true and the reasoning valid, that the atheistic premiss must be false; so, the greatest conceivable being does (and, indeed, must) exist.

We may immediately wonder quite what is meant by existence in reality being greater than existence in the understanding alone. Mind you, we do have an intuitive grasp that a million pounds in the bank is greater than an imagined million pounds.

God is that being than which nothing greater can be conceived; so let us use the term 'God' instead of the long description and consider the following step in the argument:

If God exists in the understanding alone, then we can conceive of a greater being, namely God existing in reality.

The fool's reply, though, could be that he is not suggesting that God actually exists in the understanding, but that we possess in the understanding the idea *of* God – and so, if God did exist, even necessarily, our idea would be *of* that existent. Our idea of God is no more a contender for being God than our idea of champagne is a contender for being champagne. We possess ideas of unicorns and Zeus. Were Zeus and unicorns to exist, our ideas would be of them; the ideas are no poor man versions of Zeus and unicorns.

Anselm's argument has given rise to many variants – and challenges. From the days of Kant, who rejected the argument, philosophers have bandied the slogan 'Existence is not a predicate'. That is typically taken to be saying that 'existing' is not a property of items in the way that colour, mass and size are properties. To say that certain items exist is to say that there are items as described, not to be adding a further description. When we wonder whether the Loch Ness Monster, described in a certain way, exists we are not wondering whether the monster has another property, but whether there is such a monster in reality, satisfying the description given.

Once you describe a desired object – suppose you give descriptions of ideal partners to dating agencies – existence is not a further *feature*. Existence is, though, often something presupposed – otherwise you would lack justified complaint, if the agencies produced lists of individuals satisfying your descriptions yet the individuals were all figures of fiction.

The Ontological Argument, one way or another, makes use of God as being most perfect, most perfect in that he possesses maximal reality. That maximal reality must include necessary existence. Hence, the argument concludes, God necessarily exists.

Whatever the oddness in ascribing existence, we sometimes conclude from an item's descriptions that it cannot exist. You wonder whether Squiggle exists. You then learn that Squiggle is a drawn shape that is solely circular and solely square; you rightly conclude that Squiggle lacks existence. We can work out that certain items must exist: for example, a prime number must exist between the numbers ten and twelve. Numbers and concepts, though, are abstract entities lacking causal powers; the divine being is meant to be all-powerful and no abstraction at all. It is difficult to see how any pure *a priori* reasoning could point to the existence of an item capable of causally affecting the world.

God, let us reiterate, is intended as a special case regarding *a priori* arguments. Suppose we conceive of the island than which nothing greater, nothing more perfect, can be conceived – an ironic suggestion by Gaunilo, a Benedictine monk and contemporary of Anselm. It would be ridiculous to think that, as a result, we could validly reason to the island's existence. The same goes for other hypothesized entities, such as the perfect pizza, pussycat or Santa Claus. They fail, we may argue, because there is no clear description of such proposed items. How large, lush and sunny must the perfect island be? How many purrs from the perfect pussycat? Similar questions may undermine any clear sense to understanding God as a perfect being, a being of maximal reality. Just as the number series has no greatest number – mention a number however large, and larger ones may be given – so maybe there cannot exist a being with the greatest possible power or knower of all truths.

Despite the above criticisms of the Ontological Argument, we should resist slamming it as mere word-play as is popularly done, often by evolution promoters and hasty atheists. There are genuine questions about what can be conceived, about the nature of *a priori* reasoning and of maximal reality. However, even if the Ontological Argument worked, it would solve neither the problems of the relationship between God and the universe nor the puzzles concerning the nature of God.

## Divine commands, evil and the devil

Many people rest intellectually content with the physical universe existing without a creator/designer and, when confronted

## BELIEF, FAITH – AND PASCAL'S WAGER

If you believe that eternal life will come your way, you believe that it is true that eternal life will come your way. Beliefs aim at truth: if you sincerely believe that *p*, you believe that *p* is true. Were you able to switch on beliefs at will, you would be thinking, it seems, that you could switch on the world in a certain way, as you wanted.

# Sensitivity to evidence

Because beliefs aim at truth they need to be sensitive to evidence. If you believe that it is dry outside, but then, outside, water splatters over you, you should revise your belief – or look for an explanation of how on a dry day, you got wet: maybe a neighbour hosed you down. If you believe that God is all-loving, yet you note vast gratuitous sufferings, you need either to give up the loving accolade or adjust some other belief: maybe the sufferings are in fact necessary as means to some excellent end.

Although you cannot switch on a belief, you can decide to act *as if* you believe – and you can decide simply to place trust, or have faith, in someone or something.

# Pascal's Wager

Pascal argued that it is rational to believe in God. On the one hand, if you do so believe and there is a God, you have the likelihood of eternal bliss; if there is no God, you have wasted a few Sundays through confessions and foregone some small delights. On the other hand, if you are a non-believer and there is a God, then eternal damnation threatens, the possibility of which easily swamps the non-believing pleasures and your religion-free Sundays.

That reasoning is glib, for which God, which rituals, should you support? Even if the reasoning is sound, it does not itself enable you to believe in God – for, as said, you cannot just switch on belief. You may, though, seek genuine believers, hoping that their belief is contagious. Despite unworthy initial motives, you may become a genuine believer, passing any divine test for sincere belief.

with mathematical truths, they shrug shoulders, accepting that mathematics is objective, yet not in want of divine explanation. Once they reflect on morality as objective, things change. They may insist that God is necessary as moral commander, underwriting morality's objectivity: morality implies moral law and that requires a divine law-giver. Now, the reasoning can quickly be challenged for, even assuming morality's objectivity, moral 'oughts' may no more need a law-giver than do mathematical truths.

Although God, morality and religion are often on harmonious parade, morality paradoxically poses problems for God and our concept of God – rather than God and our concept of God aiding morality. One concern, discussed for centuries, is the Euthyphro, a dilemma derived from Plato's dialogue of the same name, a dialogue between Socrates and Euthyphro. The dialogue raises a puzzle about piety and what the gods love, but the puzzle has since been wrapped round goodness and God's commands. The background belief for examination is that goodness needs to be understood as constituted by God's commands. The dilemma is thus: does God command the good if and only because it is good; or is the good, good if and only because God commands it?

Suppose, on the one hand, that the good is good if and only because God commands it. Then, whatever God commands would be good. Why, then, should we praise God for his goodness? It looks as if it is true by definition that *whatever* God commands is good. To claim that God is good would be no more substantive than claiming that bachelors are unmarried. Further, we may worry, were God to command torture, rape and pillage, then they would be acts of goodness. Suppose, on the other hand, that God commands the good if and only because it is good, then that suggests that the good exists independently of God's commands; so goodness, it seems, does not require God's existence.

We ought not complacently to accept those criticisms. Maybe sense could be made, for example, of God being identical with goodness. That, of course, generates new problems, not least what such an identity claim means, and also how goodness relates to omnipotence and omniscience. The Euthyphro dilemma should certainly remind us that it is far from obvious that moral factors point to divine existence. We may go further: moral considerations may point to the absence of God. Here is the Problem of Evil for, if God exists, and if evils are understood as unnecessary sufferings, then we are confronted by the inconsistent triad:

God is all powerful. God is all good. Evil exists.

The argument evolves thus:

Either God cannot abolish evil or he will not.
If he cannot, then he is not all powerful.
If he will not, then he is not all good.

Given that evils exist, the conclusion is that God is either not all powerful or not all good – which conflicts with much religious belief.

Suppose you are inclined to believe that the universe must have an all-powerful creator designer: you investigate the world for evidence of his character. You would surely find considerable evidence, through the unnecessary sufferings of millions of people and other animals, to blacken such a creator's name, a point emphasized by John Stuart Mill. Indeed, perhaps the universe is the result of a devilish power or of good and bad powers in conflict.

The blackening argument against an all-good, all-powerful God is not as knock-down as it may appear. We need to distinguish between moral and natural evils, the former being those deliberately inflicted by human beings, the latter resulting from non-human natural events, such as earthquakes and floods. The former exist, believers often insist, because human beings have been granted free will, a feature far more valuable than being robotic.

The 'free will defence' of the world's suffering presupposes that there is no contradiction in free agents being created by God. Now, God, it is often picturesquely suggested, chose which world to create from an infinite number of possible worlds; so, he could have created a different world with agents who freely would not inflict unnecessary sufferings. True, we may wonder why he would do that; but we may wonder all the more why he would create a world with so many unnecessary sufferings. Let us remember, God is omniscient, so he should know what his created free agents will do; and such knowledge in itself does not mean that the agents are not truly free.

Whatever we may make of the above, there remains the problem of the natural evils, of sufferings uncaused by particular human beings, but caused by climatic catastrophes. It is difficult to see what defence can be given for those, other than that the conditions and natural laws that lead to them are as necessary as mathematical truths, despite appearances to the contrary – but why believe that?

ϒ

This chapter has given but a flavour of debates concerning God's existence. For many, God is ultimately a mystery. When so, we may doubt the explanatory value of divine references in answering questions of why the universe exists and is as it is. Explanations, to be explanations, ought not to invoke further mysteries. We may as well rest content with the mystery, if one it be, of the universe's existence.

It is worth adding that even arch atheists sometimes hesitate at claiming that God does not exist. A mantra is 'You cannot prove a negative.' Now, that mantra, unless qualified, is false. Many negatives can be proved by reasoning: there are no round squares, no largest whole number. Further, you can probably prove that no elephant sits on your head as you read this book. Some argue that we cannot prove *beyond doubt* that there is no china teapot orbiting the moon (though could anything china survive such orbiting?); but that should not make us agnostic, wondering either way, about such a teapot. To be non-believers in lunar-orbiting teapots is not to rule out the possibility of error. So, too, atheists need not collapse into being agnostics, unsure about God's existence.

Atheists simply believe that there is no God; but, as Bertrand Russell quipped, if atheists do then encounter a divine designer, they should argue that he had provided insufficient evidence for rational belief in his existence. Of course, that atheistic stance assumes, as with the arguments for God above, that the concept of God is neither contradictory nor without content. Theists may themselves, indeed, be at a loss regarding quite what constitutes belief in God; as noted initially, some argue that talk of God must not be understood at all in terms of a super-natural being having existence. The god-intoxicated Spinoza would argue that consistency in reason shows that God and Nature must indeed be one and the same – and everything is necessarily as it is.

Maybe the best attitude is summed up by Charles Dunbar Broad, an early twentieth-century Cambridge philosopher, with interest in psychical research. All we can do regarding godly encounters and afterlives is wait and see or, alternatively…

Wait and not see.

# 10

# The arts: what *is* the point?

In October 1985 four Palestinian gunmen hijacked the Italian cruise liner the Achille Lauro, in the Eastern Mediterranean, with hundreds of passengers and crew members aboard. Their demand was for Israel to release fifty Palestinian prisoners, otherwise the ship and passengers would be blown sky high. Neither event happened. Negotiations ended the hijack, with safe conduct for passengers and hijackers – but only after one passenger had been shot dead: Leon Klinghoffer, a Jewish American, disabled, wheel-chair user, holidaying with his wife. His body and wheelchair had been thrown overboard.

In March 1991, *The Death of Klinghoffer*, an opera by the important American composer John Adams, was premiered. It received considerable protest from the Klinghoffer family, from some Israelis and Jews. The central complaint was that it human-ized the terrorists. As a consequence – and even after Adams made some changes – planned performances were cancelled. It has rarely been staged; its first London opera house performance was not until 2012.

$$\Upsilon$$

Artists – be they actors, authors or architects; be they painters, dancers or composers – obviously seek to affect audiences; so, ought some topics to be forbidden? Should the Klinghoffer opera be performed, despite the family's objections? The answers require evaluation of political and moral factors – of incitement dangers, the importance of free expression, yet also sensitivity to people's feelings. There are related specific questions of how, for example, music can have political impact: that music does have such impact was certainly believed by Stalin who objected to Shostakovich's compositions and what they were 'saying'. More obviously, heavy and aggressive 'rap' music with violent lyrics is unlikely to be conducive to social harmony.

Let us look at some prior related questions that arise. Note that 'art' and 'artist' are used here covering all the arts. Although philosophical discussion typically has 'high art' to the fore – paintings, poetry, lieder, opera, for example – readers may reflect to what extent the points being made apply to the 'low art' of comics, jokes, pop songs, musicals.

Quite what makes something into a work of art? What makes art good art? What, indeed, is the point of the arts? After all, were Adams' opera intended simply to give voice to the Palestinians – or Picasso's *Guernica* to speak of warfare horrors, or Jacques Louis David's painting to tell of Socrates's death – it should be assessed as are election speeches for content and effectiveness. One political objection to the opera, though, refers to the beauty of the hijackers' arias, a beauty which some interpret as honouring the terrorists. That objection reminds us that, independently of external results, particular works of art are evaluated as good or bad in themselves. They may be primarily assessed for form – in the opera cited, how the rhythms and melodies, for example, interplay with the libretto – or how form and content combine to express emotions or represent the world – or, indeed, lift our eyes to some moral truths. The assessment – as unclear as it is – is aesthetic. Yet that assessment readily leads to talk of understanding what a work of art says, and that, as seen, may mesh with real events such as terrorism, the Spanish Civil War or the death of Socrates.

Philosophy of the arts is often labelled 'aesthetics', though, as seen, it may lead into politics. The term 'aesthetic' – from the Greek for sensory perception – is used to characterize the distinctive experience, understanding and value that we associate with the arts. The term, in this modern sense, was introduced by

Kant's teacher, namely A. G. Baumgarten: he emphasized that appreciation of, for example, poetry requires appropriate sensual *perceptions* of rhythm and sound; the appreciation is not solely intellectual. Aesthetic appreciation cannot be second-hand or by third-party reports: students' study notes on *Hamlet* provide no quick aesthetic appreciation. The haunting beauty of Schubert's *Winterreise* – or the mood of a jazz improvisation or even Amy Winehouse's singing – is not gained through mere description.

Aesthetic experience – however characterized – is not all that is experienced, when experiencing art: with plays, costume costs may be the focus; with paintings, the type of canvas; with music, the conductor's furious baton waves. Further, aesthetic experience can result directly from the world, from, for example, landscapes, shades in the horse's mane, even unstable stacks of books. Aesthetic experience is not a sufficient means for identifying such items as art. Further still, providing aesthetic experiences is not necessary for something to be a work of art, though maybe it is necessary that someone offers up the work for aesthetic appraisal. Clearly, we need to reflect a little more on the identity of artworks before turning to aesthetic experience and its value.

## What is art?

Many people are at a loss, even outraged, by certain items presented as art – for example, a urinal, some bricks, and, a dishevelled bed. Marcel Duchamp's *Fontaine* is the urinal signed 'R. Mutt, 1917', intended as a joke, yet soon iconic. The bricks are Carl Andre's *Equivalent VIII*; and *My Bed* is courtesy of Tracey Emin, now – to the surprised despair of some – a Royal Academy professor of drawing. There is Kazimir Malevich's *Black Square* which consists of a black square painted on a white surround. John Cage's composition *4'33"* has a pianist sitting at a piano for (surprisingly) four minutes 33 seconds – not playing.

## WHAT DO WE APPRECIATE WHEN APPRECIATING ART?

Kazimir Malevich, *Black Square* (1913)

Those examples should remind us that currently we are considering what makes something art – not thereby good art – though assessments of value do change. At the 1913 premier of Stravinsky's *Le sacre du printemps* (*The Rite of Spring*), the music's dissonance and references to fertility rites engendered fistfights in the audience between opponents and defenders. The work is now a much admired part of mainstream orchestral work and ballet. We listen with different ears.

At least paintings in art galleries are clear cases of art – be they good or bad – or are they? The galleries' walls are painted; they manifest paintings, yet the walls are not usually considered works of art – in contrast to Michelangelo's painting on the Sistine Chapel's ceiling. Symphonies are sound sequences; so are the coughs, creaking chairs and conductors' murmurings, but they are not thereby art.

Focusing on particular paintings, people sometimes treat 'genuine' artworks as essentially representational: the painting is of a particular woman – think of the search for the sitter of the *Mona Lisa* – the drawing is of that valley yonder. Representations – newspaper, passport and wedding photographs – are not, though, usually viewed as artistic; and many abstract paintings are far from obviously representational. True, music and dance may occasionally be perceived as resembling bird song or ocean waves, but such resemblances are exceptional. Further, if representation is understood as essentially involving resemblances, then things quickly go haywire. Paintings of horses have closer resemblances to other rectangular items of colours (other paintings) than to horses. Music that represents pastoral scenes bears little resemblance to such scenes.

An objection to the above criticism is that resemblance is not key to representation. If A resembles B, then B resembles A; but if paintings represent horses, the horses do not thereby represent the paintings. Representation, it has been argued, in the artistic context is often more akin to expression, expression of emotions, moods and passions. The drawing, the dance, the string quartet's performances are not picturing anger, despair or love, but express-ing them. Leo Tolstoy, for example, in his enthusiasm for art writes thus:

> One man consciously by means of certain external signs, hands
> on to others feelings he has lived through, and others are infected
> by these feelings and also experience them.

It is as if Tolstoy thinks that the signs – the artworks – can convey the feelings. Now, certainly audiences often feel moved – dis-tressed, delighted – when watching plays, gazing at paintings or listening to music, but that alone is not what makes the works instances of art. Sensations, pleasurable or otherwise, are provided, unmediated, by warm beds and malt whisky; beds and whisky (Ms Emin's is exceptional) are not thereby art. When delighting in paintings, or moved to tears by the singing, would a syringe which produces those effects do just as well? The answer to Wittgenstein's question is 'no'. What we value are not solely experiential effects 'from within' – a point related to the moral of Chapter One's experience machine.

Returning directly to 'What is art?' a recent approach is the 'institutional': artworks are artefacts (or natural items presented as such) upon which representatives of a certain social institution – 'the art world' – have conferred a status, namely, to be appreci-ated. The institutional view immediately justifies the bricks, the silence, the dishevelled bed *et al* as art: they have received such status. The bed selected for the art gallery is an artwork; similar beds that remain outside such institutions are not. True, the painted walls are in the gallery, but they have not received the required status.

The institutional approach immediately suffers objections. What counts as the art world? What justifies the authority of its

## SHOULD ART REPRESENT?

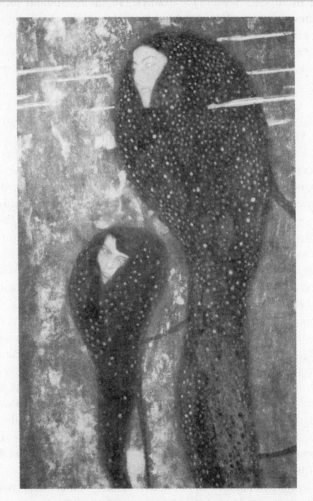

Gustav Klimt, *Nixen* (*Silberfische*), *Nymphs* (*Silver Fish*) (1899)

representatives – and upon what basis do those representatives confer artistic status? The whole approach, unless more is said, smacks of circularity: art is whatever curators consider as art. Contrast with the Nobel Prize: the status of Nobel prize-winner is conferred, but not just by anyone and not solely because the individuals are considered by the conferrers to be Nobel prize-winners.

$$\gamma$$

In the Prologue, we touched upon Wittgenstein and family resemblances. Here is the (abbreviated) source (*Philosophical Investigations* §66/67):

> Consider for example the proceedings that we call 'games'.
> I mean board-games, card-games, ball-games, Olympic Games,
> and so on. What is common to them all? –
>
> Don't say: 'There must be something common, or they would
> not be called "games" ' – but look and see whether there is any-
> thing common to all...
>
> For if you look at them you will not see something that is
> common to all, but similarities, relationships, and a whole series
> of them at that... And the result of this examination is: we see a
> complicated network of similarities overlapping and criss-cross-
> ing: sometimes overall similarities, sometimes similarities of
> detail.

Some games are competitive; some are not. Many games involve more than one player, but Patience does not. Lots of games have set rules for winning and losing, but such rules are absent when, for example, throwing a ball against a wall in play. The similarities, Wittgenstein suggests, may be summed as 'family resemblances' for family resemblances overlap and criss-cross regarding build, features, eye colour, gait, temperament and so forth.

Seeking certain definite criteria that all works of art must satisfy is arguably as foolish as searching for the commonality to all games, other than being games. We may use Wittgenstein thus:

> Consider for example what we call 'the arts' or subjects for aesthetic appraisal. I mean paintings, drawings, installations, poems, novels, plays, string quartets, ballet, opera – Le Corbusier architecture, William Morris designs, Wedgwood pottery, and so on. What is common to them all? –
>
> Don't say: 'There must be something common, or they would not be called "arts"' – but look and see whether there is anything common to all...
>
> For if you look at them you will not see something that is common to all, but similarities, relationships, and a whole series of them at that – *and so forth.*

Similarly within one art form:

> Consider for example the art found in art galleries. I mean Leonardo's *Mona Lisa*, Whistler's *Arrangement in Grey and Black No. 1*, Klimt's *Nymphs*, Picasso's *Weeping Woman* and *Guernica*, Malevich's *Black Square*, Rothko's *Red on Maroon*, even Damien Hurst's *The Physical Impossibility of Death in the Mind of Someone Living*... What is common to them all? –
>
> Don't say... *and so forth.*

When curators select items as art, worthy of display – and when people present works as works of art – a large range of considerations may be relevant, depending on the case. That observation, as well as resisting insistence that all art must possess something in common, should discourage the search for sharp dividing lines between art and non-art. To stay with art galleries, curators may be impressed by formal features – the vibrancy of colour, the interplay of shapes – or by works as developments of a tradition, or representing biblical scenes or allegories, or by what is shown about surrounding social conditions, and so forth. They may select certain items because they understand the artists as challenging a tradition or what may be viewed as works of art. We may, indeed, attend to virtually any items and point to features of possible aesthetic appraisal – for example, balance, unity, gracefulness of line, poise of movement.

With the above thoughts to the fore, where the institutional view gains some ground is that we, not unreasonably, may defer to those who are experts in the central cases – paradigm cases – in the history of art. Their selection of new works for aesthetic consideration carries some (but only some) weight. We should adopt a principle of charity – to see if there is something aesthetically valuable that we may initially be missing. After all, we defer to expert botanists regarding newly discovered species of algae.

## 'Too much salt'

Observe visitors in art galleries – what is going on? They gaze at certain paintings; they nod and point, declaring approval or disapproval, maybe indicating how, in a painting, some lines over there flow into colours over here – or how Klimt's *Nymphs* is symbolic, or Miro's painting *Kissing* looks nothing like kissing.

Watch people listening to a symphony or viewing ballet or opera. They can be absorbed; later they may speak of one movement dragging, yet another was lively and interesting, expressing a joyous feeling – how later there was an intriguing contrast between the excitement on stage, yet despair and lamentation in the music's arpeggios.

Of course, people often simply speak of enjoying the music, the exhibition, the novel. We have already argued, though, that aesthetic enjoyment is not akin to syringe-induced pleasures or those of bed and whisky unmediated. True, enjoyment – pleasures or indeed pains – sometimes arise because mediated by judgement of, for example, the aforementioned bed and whisky as scene of previous passions since lost forever; and aesthetic appreciation – the delight in art – also requires awareness, judgement, but it must be the right sort, with right connections. There is more to appreciation than desires to utter or judge 'I like it'.

Students may be delighted that they attended a play – because the play is on the examination syllabus – but they may have experienced no delight in the play. Their delight rests solely on attendance as means to a desired external end: passing the examination. Lovers may be pleased that they saw the drawings by Schiele again, but only because the works reminded them of their first erotic encounter, when in Amsterdam. Schiele's drawings, in that example, are valued as a means to an end. Contrasting with the two examples just given, aesthetic delight lies in, it has been suggested, no external end. Aesthetic appreciation rests in, what Kant labels, 'disinterest' – though certainly not 'disinterest' in the sense of uncaring.

The appreciation is disinterested for it is directed on the art objects themselves, rather than as means to external ends – such as passing examinations, useful covers for wall stains, or stimulating memories of past loves. Related to this is the thought that pure *aesthetic* appreciation needs no regard for whether objects portrayed exist in reality. Artists may be skilful in their drawings, the drawings earning the accolade 'lifelike', but that accolade arguably does not manifest disinterested aesthetic evaluation. The Klinghoffer opera, on the 'disinterest' theory, is to be evaluated in itself rather than as accurate representation of the hijacking. There is, though, a seeming caveat to 'disinterest', when art is appreciated as lifting eyes to truth, justice and virtue.

Aesthetic appreciation is also disinterested in that, according to Kant, it rests not at all on mere personal taste. Personal tastes differ; some prefer sugar in coffee, others do not. We simply accept such differences. In contrast, we may offer reasons why – and may argue about how – one song is more beautiful and more beautifully sung than another, one painting has more depth than another, one novel's characters are more convincing than another's. It would be deviant if someone truly thought dustbins more beautiful than sunsets, yet failed to explain why – for example, by appealing to the bins' subtle shadings of grey.

The Kantian idea is that art appreciation requires, paradoxically expressed, a disinterested interest. Aesthetic appreciation requires us, in the end, to focus on the work itself, on what is before us – yet what are we doing, when we do focus thus and evaluate the work?

Creative cooks, when developing recipes, may be artistic, producing new subtleties in flavour, colour combinations and presentation. Of course, therein risks danger and minor disaster: too much salt may be added. Now, here is Wittgenstein:

> What does a person who knows a good suit say when trying on
> a suit at the tailor's? 'That's the right length', 'That's too short',
> 'That's too narrow'. Words of approval play no rôle, although he
> will look pleased when the coat suits him.

Although words of approval do enter, the tailoring analogy suggests that aesthetic appreciation involves sensing whether there is a 'good fit' in the artwork – and good fit may lead to aesthetic delight and evaluation. Now, assessment of 'good fit' requires awareness of what style of suit is sought – and so, sometimes what artists intend. That latter point raises the immediate problem that often we lack knowledge of artistic intention; and, for that matter, actual intentions may be irrelevant: artists can be mistaken or deviant about their art. Some have therefore announced 'the

## MUST GOOD ART BE BEAUTIFUL?

Jacques Louis David, *The Death of Socrates* (1787)

Egon Schiele, *Der Tod und die Frau, Death and the Woman* (1915)

death of the author' – of the artist – or condemned the search for intentions as manifesting an 'intentional fallacy'. We need not embrace such extreme responses: we should accept that matters are case by case.

Artists' intentions can help guide us to see things that we should otherwise miss; yet we may also project our very own ideas of what makes a work aesthetically successful. At other times, awareness of artistic traditions, cultural surroundings, are preeminent. We frequently need relevant background knowledge and awareness, but only as aid for our seeing or hearing what is in the artwork itself. Contrasting with *relevant* background is the way in which labels and prices can affect what we 'taste' in wines – and how, on learning that paintings are forgeries, we may suddenly see them as aesthetically devalued, despite our being visually unable to spot any difference between the fake and true, a point to which we shall return.

David Hume attends to a tale in Cervantes' *Don Quixote* concerning two men who taste some hogshead wine. They find the wine very good, except that one is disturbed by a slight flavour of leather, the other irritated by a scent of iron. The men are mocked as pretentious; yet on finishing the wine, what is found at the bottom of the cask? – An old key with a leather thong.

The arts – aesthetic experiences – are valuable because they may manifest a cultivation and refinement of our senses, imagination and understanding; and, while there may be many disagreements about good art, it is false that 'anything goes', that anything is as good as anything else. Just as some people are colour blind, hopeless at algebra or unmoved by animals' suffering, so some are aesthetically blind, bad at hearing a poem's beauty, or unmoved by the poignancy of a cello sonata.

We may now see how 'low art' to 'high art' forms a spectrum. At the low art level – the pop song, the formulaic 'colouring by numbers' painting – little is to be discovered by listening or seeing; the scope is scant for imaginative involvement. There is lack of subtlety, of feeling that 'something is being said' by the form. Of course, words in fiction – be they formulaic love stories or atmospheric plays by Samuel Beckett – are used to say something; but aesthetic appeal rests in large part on the form – economy of expression, how characters are drawn, scenes described – and how that form encourages us to enter the world portrayed.

## From Afghan hounds to fakes

Much is said about paintings, music and literature, when audiences and critics attempt to explain, challenge or endorse particular aesthetic attractions; yet if we seek justification for the descriptions deployed, we may be baffled. The lines in the drawing are too heavy; the adagio is light-hearted; the novel is dark and brooding – yet it is not *literally* the case that lines are heavy, adagios light-hearted, and novels dark and brooding. We should not, though, dismiss such terms. After all, a woman who is heavy-hearted is not literally heavy in heart and, when you have butterflies in your stomach, no butterflies are there now; for that matter they never have been.

Consider a simple case of describing a sound as 'low'. Is the sound really akin to a low ceiling or mood? The violin playing in Vaughan Williams' *The Lark Ascending* readily puts us in mind of a skylark soaring high in the sky; yet what similarity exists between the 'high' notes and a bird's flight and height?

Continuing the focus on music, whether we have knowledge of the underlying musical analysis or not, we are often minded to speak of music as expressive. Yet, as noted, the music obviously is not itself a person, so it cannot be wistful, sad or lamenting – and who knows what the composers' moods were (perhaps the composers were irritated or hungry, be it for food or for payment)?

Consider the Afghan hound: its appearance strikes us as aloof and dignified – yet the hound is no more aloof than a face in the clouds is menacing. Some would argue that features of the Afghan's stance and movements resemble features of aloof people. So, too, maybe wistful music is described as such because it puts us in mind of the wistfulness of acquaintances. Of course, the music does not 'look' wistful; but the way in which it moves, its contours, it may be suggested, resemble the contours, the movements, the facial expressions, of wistful people.

Music that we recognize as expressing a mood or emotion need not thereby cause that mood or emotion within us. We may, though, experience emotional reactions to the music as we would to friends expressing the emotions. After all, we may find it difficult not to feel sorry for the basset hound with its drooping face, despite knowing how silly that reaction is.

We naturally extend the use of words in certain directions – and extending certain descriptions to artworks is arguably no more mysterious than the other extensions just mentioned. That is not to deny that we may seek explanations for those extensions; it is not to deny the mystery of what constitutes our appreciating or understanding music and paintings. Our human capacity to find similarities is, indeed, intriguing.

A related 'expressive' puzzle is the fact that we can be moved into our own emotional expression by fictional characters, despite knowing them fictional and non-existent. Audiences can be brought to tears when heroines are betrayed by lovers, when the mother loses her child – and they may long to shriek out warnings to the innocents unwittingly heading into a trap. All the time, the viewers are in the comfort (or maybe discomfort) of the theatre or home armchairs; the action is taking place on stage or in film – yet even after the ending, audiences sometimes continue to worry and wonder what happens next.

In understanding what is going on, we face a dilemma. If we stress the reality of the viewers' concerns and beliefs, then surely they should be jumping out of their seats to save the victims; if we stress their knowledge that it is all make-believe, then why the tears, the concern, the distress – tears, concern and distress directed at *fictional* entities? They are not, though, make-believe tears; and the emotions can feel real enough. Perhaps that just shows how irrational we can be; yet the most rational of people undergo those feelings despite knowing that they are participating in fiction.

We need to reflect that the very thought of things can generate emotions, without the need for full belief or disbelief. We may be upset by imaginary disasters happening to loved ones, even though we know that they are only imagined and will not happen. Maybe that is sufficient to show how we should handle our reactions to fiction. We do not really believe that the heroines are being harmed; rather the mere thought, the imaginative awareness, of their harm is sufficient to generate our pity, our tears. The play, the novel – and our imaginative involvement – bring forth real emotions. That is the way we are built.

What goes on when we understand and appreciate music is puzzling, yet there are similar puzzles with paintings and drawings. Even life-like paintings are not usually meant to mislead us into thinking that what is represented is actually present. True, a *trompe l'oeil*, suitably positioned, may lead us to reach for an apple that it not there, but representational art typically fascinates us for what we can 'see in' the painting, well aware that it is a painting. Recall, in Chapter One, how even a simple line drawing may be seen as a duck, then as a rabbit. Somehow splashes of paint on canvases enable us to 'see in' the works three dimensional physical objects as well as emotions and expressions. Even abstract paintings – Malevich's, Rothko's, Pollock's – lead us to see colours hovering over or behind others (whether or not paints were applied in that order), shining through as moods and emotions.

As said earlier, background is relevant to our aesthetic appreciation, yet that appreciation must end with its focus on the works themselves. If that is so, then we meet the puzzle of forgeries. Can there be any justification for altering our aesthetic evaluation of works, if discovered to be fakes? True, fakes are often inferior works, but consider a case where, say, the sole differences between the genuine Picasso and a fake Picasso are factors concerning chemical composition, date of origination and so forth. Aesthetically, it seems, there is no difference.

Some argue that moral evaluations enter here. The fake is witness to deception: some dubious practices of 'passing off' have occurred. Yet why should that matter aesthetically? In any case, let us suppose that, in our Picasso example, a genuine misattribution has occurred: intentional deception was absent.

Well, the fake before us lacks relevant historical associations with Picasso's brush-strokes. The paint was not applied by Picasso. Such causal connections are often valuable to us. Witness the importance of wearing not a replica but the very ring given by your mother – or holding the original score by Schubert rather than a copy. Yet, why should such associations in our Picasso example possess *aesthetic* importance? In answer, we could argue that the artist's creativity being displayed in the painting is part of what we value: forgers are skilled but lack artistic originality. Even that, though, demands qualification: a so-called forger could be working creatively in the manner of Picasso's 'blue period' as Picasso did himself.

A related puzzle is the ontological – the reality – status of works of art. We first approach it through music. Quite what *is* Schubert's song-cycle *Winterreise*? We hear different performances of the cycle; but what is the cycle? It is not the original manuscript: that could be lost, yet the cycle would not thereby be lost. The song-cycle would seem to be neither a physical object on paper nor sound vibrations of particular performances, but rather a *type* of entity neither in space nor time, yet somehow the source of different spatio-temporal performances, of different *tokens* of that type. The same applies to novels and poems – and even to paintings and engravings where artists have happily churned out copies of their own work, according to demand. Of course many paintings are unique, without complexities of production-line copies – for example, the *Mona Lisa* is unique – yet are we right to think of the *Mona Lisa* as *that* particular physical object in the Louvre? Suppose it were possible to create perfect copies, indistinguishable from the original… That may suggest that even a painting needs to be understood as a type, a type usually manifested in just one token. The importance of the type/token distinction was seen earlier regarding the identity theory of mind.

## Aesthetic value, beauty and love

With certain paintings, music and poems – with some buildings – we return to experiencing them time and again, delighting in the repeated experiences or in similar performances. It is doubtful whether we are thereby always discovering something new, but undoubtedly we find their form meaningful, of value. We should challenge any assumption that for works to be meaningful and valuable, we must be able to put adequately into words what constitutes their meaning and value. Just to say that these paintings or those quartets, for example, are poignant is to say far, far less than the paintings and quartets themselves. If the music could be put into words, why bother with the music? Two friends who value their friendship – the friendship gives meaning to their lives – are not thereby enabled to express that meaning in words.

The apparent disinterested aspect of aesthetic appreciation may establish one quick value for the arts – namely, reminding us that some things must have intrinsic value and are not valued as means to an end. That may also remind us of the importance of play and playfulness – of the *ludic* – in life and in art. Artists play with creating imaginary worlds or new perspectives on this world. We, the spectators, let our imaginations play: we may dance to the rhythms heard in the music and seen in the paintings.

Play, playfulness and aesthetic appreciation naturally suggest a delight: yet some art deliberately sets out to disturb and does so successfully. It is almost grotesque to speak of delighting in Picasso's *Guernica* or Adams's *Klinghoffer* or David's *Death of Socrates*, in view of the subject-matter; and while we may casually speak of enjoying Britten's opera of a brooding death in Venice or a Shakespeare tragedy or Schiele's anguished eroticism, this may often be but a way of expressing our recognition of moral dilemmas or the bleakness of the human condition.

Acknowledging the disinterested interest in aesthetic evalua- tion is not to deny that works of art may make us see the real world in a new light, under new perspectives – as do religious texts for some people. Certain works may inspire us to live lives differently – and, in so doing, may have moral impact on what sort of people we seek to become. That may explain why some identify with harmony in certain artworks, whereas others feel more at home with tensions, morbidity or 'life on an edge' – and others lose themselves under the mesmerizing spell of Philip Glass's *Satyagraha* and other 'minimalist' music and art. That is also where a special place may arise for beauty in art.

Beauty inspires us – and even when encountering the haunting despair of certain paintings by Munch or Schiele, or Fischer-Dieskau's singing of Schubert's *Winterreise*, or plays by Samuel Beckett, we may yet see beauty in the bleakness. Let us pursue beauty a little further.

G. E. Moore, in his 1903 *Principia Ethica*, lists some intrinsic goods, some intrinsic values, notably the passionate contempla- tion of, and communion with, beloved persons and objects of beauty. Beauty, be it found in landscapes, drawings or music, has often been understood as freeing us from earthly desires, anguishes and battles for survival. Plato lifts our eyes to the form of the

## BLOOMSBURY, BEAUTY AND MOORE

Philosophers and artists have a mixed relationship. Plato, although a literary master, sought to banish artists from his ideal state, The Republic, or at least censor them – for they may lead us away from the reality of the eternal Forms, such as Beauty, Justice, Virtue. In contrast, the pessimistic Schopenhauer (1788–1860) saw aesthetic perception as enabling us to lose ourselves – indeed, to become aware of those very Platonic realities.

**G. E. Moore** (1873–1958) is closer to home. At Cambridge, Bertrand Russell encouraged Moore into philosophy and Moore encouraged Russell into some common sense. Moore possessed 'an exquisite purity'; he became, in a sense, the secular high priest of the Bloomsbury Group, of Virginia Woolf, E. M. Forster, Roger Fry, John Maynard Keynes *et al*. Moore glorified intrinsic values of the private life, of love, of relationships, of aesthetic experiences. In contrast to Keynes's economics, Moore was unmotivated by social ideals, rights and welfare reform. Those ideals were mere means whereby people became free to realize the intrinsic goods. As Keynes later wrote, members of the group were water-spiders gracefully skimming a stream, in little contact with eddies and currents beneath.

**Two possible worlds** were described by Moore; neither contained any conscious beings. One consisted of landscapes of beauty; the other of rubbish and ugliness. It is, claimed Moore, self-evident that the former is of greater value than the latter, objectively so. Of course, that is controversial: we readily question the objectivity of aesthetic values – 'beauty is in the eye of the beholder' – yet we certainly do recognize standards within aesthetic judgement. A garden gnome, the author's singing, and certain conceptual art are far removed from beauty.

**Bertrand Russell** (1872–1970), logician and philosopher, famous for *Principia Mathematica*, for his political activism, atheism, wit, and support of 'free love', tells of a logical subterfuge. 'Moore,' he asked, 'do you always speak the truth?' 'No,' replied Moore. Now, had Russell trapped this man of utter integrity into telling a lie?

Beautiful, abstracted from all instances of beauty, as if – contrary to Wittgenstein's family resemblance approach – all beautiful items possess something in common. Our gaze on the beautiful, as beautiful, is disinterested: there is no interest of ours that the beautiful serves.

Moore's praised values of beauty and friendship – and this may surprise – possess much in common. Consider whether an item is replaceable. You may want a glass of wine – or a plumber. Any will do, so long as they have the desired features. The wine needs to be a merlot; the plumber reliable, with plumbing know-how. Once features have been set – size, price and quality – any individual with those features satisfy the wants. Contrast that replaceability with our attitudes to friends, lovers – and works of art. You may just want sex – anyone will do – and your appetite may be quickly quelled; but your sexual desire, as love, as *eros*, is directed towards the particular person: not anyone will do. Kant displayed a misunderstanding of sexual desire, when likening it to appetite: when the appetite is stilled, he wrote, 'the person is cast aside as one casts away a lemon which has been sucked dry'.

In a true friendship, in love, the friend, the lover, is not replaceable. In such cases, that particular person is essential to the relationship: his or her singularity fascinates. We value being with friends and lovers, learning of their thoughts and attitudes and, when *eros* also calls, exploring their embodiment. We value them in themselves – as we do beautiful works of art. True, we may simply find beauty in the contours of a hand – as a biological blob – but the beauty we may see in a *person* is not that of a biological blob, but of an autonomous agent mysteriously embodied.

Beauty moves us, whether found in a lover, raging ocean or string quartet. Plato, as said, directs us to the vision of heavenly forms, the form of the Beautiful, of Truth, of Justice. While Plato's understanding possesses mystical attractions, following his lead into the abstract would draw us away from the irreplaceability that we surely feel, down here on Earth, when contemplating beautiful objects or engaging with friends and lovers. Such objects, friends and lovers would be, for Plato, but means or aids to the Beautiful: any others, it seems, would do just as well.

To be true to our experiences, we find beauty in the particular. Understanding how that discovery comes about – and in what it is constituted – is itself a mystery. The lover, the friend, the performance of a favourite song cycle – we relish being in their presence. We may delight in discovering connections – how, for example, David's *Death of Socrates* relates to Satie's music *Socrate* and Plato's portrayal of Socrates in *Phaedo*; how the theme of *Death and the Maiden* occurs in poetry, in plays, in Schubert's lieder and quartets, in Schiele's paintings.

We typically delight in sharing aesthetic experiences with others, as we also delight in sharing through discussion, argument and play – and often not because of any external end in view. E. M. Forster's 'Only connect' may resonate here. The more we connect with people, the more chance we may have to lift eyes, to feel for each other, to inspire each other. Friends, lovers – and the arts – engage our disinterested curiosity.

Curiosity prefaced this book – and so, this could be a good place to end. But the Epilogue gives us one further philosophical spin at some of life's curiosities.

# Epilogue:
## mortality, immortality and the meaning of life

Samuel Pepys, with eyesight fading, wrote within the last few lines of his diary for 31st May 1669:

> And thus ends all that I doubt I shall ever be able to do with my own eyes in the keeping of my journall, I being not able to do it any longer, having done now so long as to undo my eyes almost every time that I take a pen in my hand...

Pepys reminds us of what we know so well: that our senses fail, our lives draw to a close, and our eyes on the world eventually close. One day, they close for good.

Quite what is it that we value when we value anything? Pepys valued keeping a diary, leaving his thoughts and his windings through life for others to read, for posterity. Maybe we can hear the regret, the sadness, in his voice that no longer will he be able to have such intimacies with the ink, page and words. Pepys wanted to continue writing; but he could not.

That life has an end generates melancholic musings for most of us at some stage of life. That life has an end devalues life and makes it meaningless or pointless – well, so it may seem. As a result, many hope that the end on Earth is not truly the end, though our earlier discussions on the mind and personal identity manifested some bewilderment at eternal disembodied existence. We may magnify the bewilderment by wondering how eternal life, were it a reality, helps in giving meaning to life. So, we turn to some thoughts about the meaning of life, before raising related matters of death, value and perspectives held.

## What is the point?

Talk of life's meaning engages questions such as 'What's the point, purpose, aim?' The questions are often accompanied with world-weary sighs of 'Why?' Now, points and purposes exist within lives: you move seats to escape the loud music; you wear the confident smile to fool the police. Items – corkscrews, cars and continental breakfasts – are made for a purpose, be they fit or not. In all such cases, the meaning, the point, the purpose, refers us to something further on, something other than the items in want of meaning. We may, therefore, push further, 'But what is the point, the purpose of that – of escaping the noise, of fooling the police; of opening the wine, of eating a light breakfast?' If tempted to push, we should probably find fresh resting places of 'Well, they are what I want or need; they help make me happy.'

That 'happy' answer links us to Aristotle; he spoke of everyone ultimately aiming at some good and that good is happiness, happiness being ultimately valued. Now, from everyone aiming at some good, contrary to the impression from Aristotle, it does not follow that there exists just one good at which everyone aims. That inference manifests a logical fallacy, the 'fallacy of a quantifier shift': there is a locational shift of the quantifiers 'every' and 'some'. The fallacy is seen in the move from the truth that every child was born of a woman to the falsehood that there is some woman who bore every child, that is, who bore all children.

Returning to the point, some continue with further pointed questions. 'But what is the point of happiness – or, for that matter, of reading novels, engaging in romance or having children?' When the questioning persists, some are beguiled by absurd claims that our ultimate purpose is to replicate our genes – absurd because few people, if any, have that purpose and certainly our genes do not, whatever myths and popular commentators say. Evolution may account for our existence, but does not imply that our existence is for a purpose, fit or otherwise.

When the questioning persists, we may find ourselves seeking a purpose behind all life, all creation. Here, God and eternal life may be wheeled in; but there is a strong bar to the wheeling. If a satisfactory answer to 'What is the point of X?' needs reference to something other than X, and something that does not circle back to X, then we are forever inconsolable. Even if there is a God, even if life is eternal, the same persistent questioning should arise: 'What is the point of God, of eternal life?' As Wittgenstein sceptically asked, 'Is some riddle solved by my surviving for ever?'

Disquiet manifested by 'What's the point?' arises because certain underlying assumptions ensure that no answer counts as good enough. The quest is for something as impossible as a square circle. We need to challenge the assumption that if X points to nothing outside X, then X is pointless in the sense of 'deficient'. The number seven lacks point; virtue lacks colour. They are not, thereby, deficient, lacking something possible for them. Neither seven nor virtue is the kind of thing that can have point or colour. The totality of things is not in the realm of being pointed or pointless. The general point is that points must come to an end just as, as seen elsewhere, explanations must come to an end.

## VANITY OF VANITIES

Philosophers and poets sometimes remind us of how our achievements, however great on Earth, will come to nothing. Here is Shelley:

> And on the pedestal these words appear:
> 'My name is Ozymandias, king of kings:
> Look on my works, ye Mighty, and despair!'
> Nothing beside remains. Round the decay
> Of that colossal wreck, boundless and bare
> The lone and level sands stretch far away.

Yet, Lucretius – we met him in Chapter Three – encourages us not to regret:

> Why do you weep and wail over death? If the life you have lived till now has been a pleasant thing – if all its blessings have not leaked away like water poured into a cracked pot and run to waste unrelished – why then, you silly creature, do you not retire from life's banquet as a guest who has had his fill of life...?

And he recommends the following:

> Look back at the eternity that passed before we were born, and mark how utterly it counts to us as nothing. This is a mirror that Nature holds up to us, in which we may see the time that shall be after we are dead. Is there anything terrifying in the sight – anything depressing – anything that is not more restful than the soundest sleep?

In response to Lucretius, we may feel that we have not received our fill of life – and, while we can readily make sense of how our lives could continue longer than they will, it is not easy to make sense of our lives having started many years earlier than they in fact did. Bearing in mind the radically different experiences a so-called 'you' would have undergone from birth, had 'you' been born in ancient Greece, whatever could make that ancient Greek life the early stage of your life now?

The end is sometimes within our lives. You may give point or meaning to your life through activities that you value, perhaps through nurturing your children, helping victims of torture, or simply in aesthetic appreciation. The point of your creation may have been your parents' desire for family life, a saviour child for a sibling, or an additional employee for their chimney-sweeping ventures. Those examples alert us to the thought that even if we are part of a greater purpose, even a divine purpose, that fact may provide *us* with no point or good to our lives. Witness the red grouse: they are allowed to breed as part of a greater plan – for the Glorious Twelfth and the shooting season.

We find meaning in our lives when engaged in activities that we value – yet that value does not, or, at least, should not, reside solely in the satisfactions we receive. Were satisfactions the ultimate point, then consider investing in itching powder and back-scratcher, with the following instructions:

Sprinkle the itching powder; hence you have an itch and desire
to be satisfied.
Apply the back scratcher and scratch.
Repeat.

Although we should have numerous satisfactions, the example – derived from Plato – demonstrates a simple truth: some desires are not worth much. A life consisting solely of back-scratching satisfactions would be a life with little value, unless (bizarrely) the scratching formed part of a worthwhile project, maybe a religious ritual or community bonding. Consider how we pity individuals who have become so brain-damaged that, unaware of their state, of their loss, they are completely contented, even pleased, with simply watching a ceiling's flashing light. We rightly feel that there could be more to their lives. Recall Chapter Four with Mill's resistance to swinish contentment: 'tis better to be a dissatisfied Socrates than a satisfied pig.

Our desire for X is not typically what makes X desirable; after all, why seek out X, if all that can be said in its favour is that we desire it? We usually need items to possess features that make them worthy of desire, features other than merely being desired. Sometimes that feature may be solely that X gives us pleasure, but usually not.

## Immortality, death and tedium

Schopenhauer, the nineteenth-century philosopher of pessimism, saw human life, a life of desire, as inevitably filled with suffering. His argument, sketchily presented, is that either you desire something and hence you are pained in trying to achieve that something, of not yet having your desire satisfied – or you have succeeded in satisfying your desire, but now boredom takes over and new desires are formed. The image is of Sisyphus of Greek mythology, condemned eternally to rolling a boulder to a mountain top, only to suffer its rolling back down, eternally so. For Schopenhauer, even if Sisyphus freely manages the rolling, perhaps building a mountain-top temple, he would have no improved life: he would then be bored, needing to turn to another task – and another...

Arguably, Schopenhauer's approach fails to recognize that we are not so single-minded; we usually have a diversity of interlocking activities. The approach also errs in enforcing too strongly a separation between means and ends. We often value the means as well as the ends. Human life would not be human if we secured our ends without means and hence without temporal spans. Consider how odd it would be, were every want immediately satisfied, every line of reasoning having the conclusion immediately present. We seek to achieve things; and achievements may be valued not only because of ends sought, but also because of the means, hopes and expectations.

Examination passes are no great achievements, if by luck and without work.

The above comments are far from the spirit of the media age where instant news, instant gratifications, are demanded. Maybe that spirit encourages a feeling of pointlessness for struggles form part of a meaningful life – well, at least when those struggles are for ends chosen rather than desperate attempts just to remain alive. Indeed, some devalue Mozart, *qua* achiever, because, it seems, composition came so easily to him.

Awareness of valuable achievements and states should help us to resist despair at life. Mortality, though, may still oppress. We typically seek more of what we value rather than less. Not merely do we value the beautiful landscape, the philosophical enterprise, the music – all may persist long after we have gone – we also value our awareness of them. So, although we may accept that immortality does not confer meaning on life, we may yet believe that immortality is preferable to mortality: potentially, immortality gives us more of what we value and hence, it may be claimed, more value.

To assess that suggested preference, we need knowledge of how the immortality runs. Is it embodied life on Earth and its planetary successors or some form of disembodied yet personal existence? If the immortality is disembodied, then there are the metaphysical perplexities of our identity and individuation, as discussed in Chapter Three. Further, suppose a personal disembodied existence possible: what would fill such a life? Presumably it would consist of thoughts and memories – and maybe some telepathic discourse with other disembodied beings. Perhaps it would lapse into reflections solely on abstractions, on virtue and triangles. That may lack personal appeal.

How would immortal life fare, were it embodied here on Earth? Here is a literary approach.

# The Makropulos Case

The tale tells of Emilie Marty – E. M. – who received the elixir of life over three hundred years ago. She now looks in her early forties. After those three hundred years – of being around forty – E. M. has had enough of life. She has become more of a 'case', an object, scarcely human, she thinks. She has been differently named over the decades: Elina Makropulos, Ellian McGregor, Emilia Marty. She desires death – which she eventually finds. The tale is Karel Čapek's play, later Janáček's opera.

E. M. is the sole could-be immortal. She has seen friends, children, lovers come and go. She has experienced a gamut of diverse relationships with different people, aware that they would die, while she lived on. Her great, great grandsons, unwittingly, at times sought to seduce her. Boredom and despair are to the fore. The elixir has become a curse.

If, in contrast to E. M., your own earthly immortal life was shared with a few other immortals – those sufficiently wealthy to afford elixirs – arguably you would be a species apart from regular mortals. If, in a different scenario, numerous people are immortal, then eventual 'lack of space' for newly created people must mean that male-female relationships would alter: desires for children would need cessation.

Those thoughts highlight that life immortal – and not for just three hundred years – needs details for sensible evaluation. Elixirs that confer immortality, for example, must presumably protect people from significant harms and death. Such immortal lives would be radically different from the mortal, with no need to worry about earthquakes, floods and nuclear weapons. People could cross roads without looking. Deployment of concepts such as courage, patience and risk would radically differ from the current. Presumably immortal albeit biological bodies would be constituted very differently: would immortals still need and want to eat and drink? Or is the idea just that of non-aging?

Once immortal embodied living is properly described, even if possessive of sense, it may lack appeal – as with disembodied immortality, if sense can be made of that.

Whether embodied or disembodied, there are some worthwhile experiences, it may be argued, which could be repeated infinitely. If fascinated by numbers, your infinite time could be filled with never-ending reflections on yet higher numbers. Maybe, as in certain drugged hazes, you could encounter imaginary scenes and heightened sensations, returning eternally, or listen to the same music, literally endlessly. Or could you? During his mental crisis in 1826, John Stuart Mill was tormented by the thought of the exhaustibility of beautiful combinations of sounds, of nothing new.

Awareness of limits can distress – and what may also distress is the thought that therefore a long life must undergo considerable repetition. We may speculate further, regarding whether there exists a finite number of interesting sentence constructions out of the alphabet which, if all appropriately asserted and grasped, would put an end to curiosity.

Even if the boredom and horror of 'no end' could be avoided, what motivation would there be to do anything? If something could be put off until tomorrow, why not put it off? With no end in view, unless we repeatedly deceived ourselves into believing otherwise, there would be an absence of structure to life. Maybe, as E. M. came to realize, death is necessary, paradoxically, for life not to lose value. In the words of Seneca, 'He will live badly who does not know how to die well.'

Death – together with birth – provides a framework within which to pattern a life. We may wonder how a life can be evaluated as desirable or not, if we lack conception of its end. That vague thought gives rise to another: maybe life should be viewed as a work of art in progress, one that needs attention to its completion. Such thoughts possess obvious implications regarding the value of permitting suicide and euthanasia. Such thoughts also remind us that life's shape is important.

Suppose, what is probably impossible, that we could count units of value in a life: to linger on for trillions of years with one unit of value each year would generate more overall value than ninety years with a thousand units each year, if simply summed. Most of us would probably recognize the ninety years as more valuable. A short life lived brightly seems more meaningful than a long life managing just a tiny value each year. We probably also prefer a life that develops its well-being over one that commences with considerable well-being, yet thereafter constantly declines, even if the latter overall, by simple addition, gives more units of value. Shape, structure and ending are important factors in flourishing.

The above observations are not remotely intended to suggest that all is well with regard to the typical life-span. Further, whatever the typical life-span, death is likely to occur either too early or too late. For E. M. it was too late. We know well that it may be too early. To pick up a logical quantifier thread, another illegitimate shift is the following. On each day that would be our day of death, we may well desire an extra day of life. It does not follow that we therefore desire an immortal life. That may be just what we do not desire, even though our daily desires, if satisfied, would have that immortal and unwelcome outcome.

## Melancholic vapours

When finding meaning to life – to our lives – we may be readily transported by images of relishing love and friendship, music and paintings. Transported thus, we close our eyes to the sufferings of millions. That exhibits one incongruity or absurdity in life – between those that have and those that have not. Human that we are, we cannot – or, at least, arguably, should not – bracket off the world's miseries. 'Only connect' is the injunction from E. M. Forster – and we are connected to others whether we like it or not.

'All things conspire' appeared in our Preface regarding philosophical problems. However much we may seek to think otherwise, our lives are intermeshed with, conspire with, others across the seas and continents; our well-being depends in part on the radically poor existence of others, be they children working in appalling conditions in cheap clothing factories or labourers on plantations. Writing a book of philosophy, reading a book of philosophy, are luxuries – valuable activities – unavailable to the vast majority.

John McTaggart Ellis McTaggart, a Cambridge philosopher of the early twentieth century, owned a cat, Pushkin. In the cold Fen winter winds, Pushkin would have pride of place before the glowing fire, while McTaggart shivered in the corner, deep in metaphysics. McTaggart summed matters thus, 'That's the best it gets for a cat.' Pushkin was in no position to philosophize, detaching himself from his feline perspective. McTaggart, though, could reason: he could evaluate the feline life; he could step back from appearances. And he – and we – can step back, detach ourselves, or so it appears, from our own human perspective.

Seeing ourselves in a detached way may cloud our lives with melancholy vapours. Let us argue about beauty and truth as much as we like, but a little voice may urge, 'What does it all matter?' We are but specks in the universe and from the universe's viewpoint we matter not at all. At times we become worked up about our lives – about loves, careers and the greying hair – yet they lack cosmic importance. How absurd that we should see things as mattering!

We should be unimpressed by the exclamation. Suppose you constituted the whole universe in both space and time, you could still wonder why anything matters. Size is not the rub; contingencies may be. We are at the mercy of fortunes and misfortunes.

There is a curious belief – often displayed by management gurus and the America ethos – that everything can be fixed: we can achieve whatever we want, if only we try hard enough.

That is as ridiculous as thinking the world is throughout wonderful and benign. The human condition nearly always involves tragedy, be it through our own decline, aging and loss of faculties, or through decline of friends and awareness of the suffering millions. Those horrors should make us realize how fortunate we are when events go well. Even then, if sensitive, we should not, to repeat, close eyes to how our good fortunes rest in part on the misfortunes of others – and that our good fortunes largely (if not totally) are just that: matters of good fortune.

Human that we are, however detached we may try to become, it matters to us how our lives go. It also can matter how others see us. Sartre drew attention to the Other: once we are no more, we are prey to the living, to the Other. The living can categorize us, assess us and evaluate us. Before we draw our last breath though, we have the opportunity to rework our lives, casting them in new lights. Our future choices can affect how our past is perceived. The position on the chess board looks bad, but whether it is deemed bad depends, in the end, on its contribution to the eventual outcome.

♈

Philosophy is the love of wisdom and wisdom is meant to be beyond mere cleverness and knowledge; it is meant to open eyes to what is important, to meaning, to values. Now, most academic philosophers these days, in their academic labours, rarely reach or even try to reach such eye-opening understanding; they may even question what constitutes that understanding.

Wittgenstein tells of passing a bookshop where, in the window, were portraits of Russell, Freud and Einstein. Further on, in a music shop, he saw portraits of Beethoven, Schubert and Chopin. Comparing those portraits, he 'felt intensely the terrible degeneration that had come over the human spirit in the course of only a hundred years'.

## WITTGENSTEIN: A PHILOSOPHER'S LIFE

**Ludwig Wittgenstein** (1889–1951) has appeared throughout this work. He anguished about logic, ethics and life. As with Socrates, Spinoza and Kierkegaard, his life and philosophy intermeshed. Philosophy was a working on oneself. Aware of his loathsome side, he sought improvement – eventually finding some intellectual modesty.

**Life:** Wittgenstein came from a wealthy, highly cultured, Viennese family of Jewish origins, in contact with composers, angst and painters (Klimt, for one). Wittgenstein was to give away his wealth, adopting an austere life. Russell's mathematics led him into philosophy. Abandoning engineering he turned up on Russell in Cambridge, in 1911, unannounced. Russell quickly saw him as a genius.

In World War I, Wittgenstein enlisted in the Austrian army, demanding the front-line – to see whether he was to live or die – and worked on his *Tractatus Logico-Philosophicus*. In 1929, the *Tractatus* already praised, he underwent the ritual of a viva with Russell and Moore. Moore wrote, '...Mr. Wittgenstein's thesis is a work of genius; but, be that as it may, it is certainly well up to the standard required for the Cambridge degree of Doctor of Philosophy.'

Back in Cambridge in the '30's, helped by Keynes, and criticisms from F. P. Ramsey and the economist Sraffa, Wittgenstein started afresh, still sure that philosophical problems arose through language, but coming to see language as a bag of tools, with different uses: see his great posthumous *Philosophical Investigations* (1953).

**The mystical:** Wittgenstein's early work inspired the Vienna Circle – the logical positivists – in their insistence that propositions must be verifiable or falsifiable, otherwise nonsense. They had ignored the *Tractatus*'s words towards the end:

> There are, indeed, things that cannot be put into words. They *make themselves manifest*. They are what is mystical.

For Wittgenstein, what could not be said was more important than what could be. To that enigma, Ramsey quipped – aware of Wittgenstein's whistling – that it could not be whistled either.

Perhaps what is most important in life cannot be put into words. Perhaps we should take seriously Wittgenstein's final proposition in his *Tractatus*:

Whereof one cannot speak, thereof one must be silent.

♈

Friedrich Nietzsche danced in contradictions, looking beyond the mere technical analysis. He gave a vivid, but nonsensical, way for you – for me, for all of us – to judge of our lives. Please suspend belief with regard to the sense of his supposition. Instead, try to accept the possibility and suggestion at face value, even at controversial face value. Here it comes:

What if, some day or night, a demon were to steal into your loneliest loneliness and say to you:

*This life as you now live it and have lived it, you will have to live once again and innumerable times again; and there will be nothing new in it, but every pain and every joy and every thought and sigh and everything unspeakably small or great in your life must return to you, all in the same succession and sequence – even this spider and this moonlight between the trees, and even this moment and I myself. The eternal hourglass of existence is turned over again and again, and you with it, speck of dust!*

Would you not throw yourself down and gnash your teeth and curse the demon who spoke thus? ...

Or how well disposed would you have to become to yourself and to life – *to long for nothing more fervently* than this ultimate eternal confirmation and seal?

No mere melancholy vapours, but deep anguish and despair may sweep over us, if we pretend our lives as possessed of eternal repetition. 'Curiosity' is scarcely adequate as a summary of the philosophical impulse, when we reflect deeply upon what should fill our lives – how we should live our lives – when one day they will be gone, gone for good, when, indeed, it is highly likely that one day all lives, all consciousness, will be gone and gone for good – or for ill. We must live with transiency.

Suppose though, just suppose as best you can, your life – *as you now live it* – were to be repeated eternally, exactly the same each time round. Well, would you throw yourself down, gnash your teeth at the supposition of your eternal recurrence? Can your life, your values, your loves, bear eternity?

♈

And so it is that we return to Socrates and the beginnings of Western Philosophy over two thousand years ago:

The unexamined life is not worth living.

# Notes and further reading

General philosophy recommendations are in the Prologue notes. Where references or quotation sources are readily available – often on-line or in many published editions – the notes are uncluttered with publication details.

## Prologue: take your time

A substantial collection of classic and modern classic texts, 800 pages worth, containing key extracts covering all this book, is John Cottingham's *Western Philosophy: an anthology*, 2nd, edn, 2008. That is the book for you if you want important extracts. Two comprehensive, weighty, and solid undergraduate introductions to all the main areas of philosophy are edited by A. C. Grayling, *Philosophy: a guide through the subject* and *Philosophy 2: further through the subject* (1995 and 1998).

For readers unenthusiastic about weighty volumes, try, as a modern classic and slender introduction, Bertrand Russell, *The Problems of Philosophy* (first published in 1912). For accessible works of considerable influence, see the early dialogues of Plato, some under the title *The Last Days of Socrates*, and Descartes' hugely influential classic, *Meditations on First Philosophy*.

For lovers of screen reading or printing off, use the highly reliable and freely available online *Stanford Encyclopaedia of Philosophy*; and try too online Royal Institute of Philosophy.

Philosophy papers, videos of interviews and lectures are often available at university websites and on YouTube.

# Chapter One: What is it to be human?

The experience machine appeared in Robert Nozick's *Anarchy, State and Utopia*. Descartes' evil genius appeared in Descartes' *Meditations* (1 and II). Plato's Allegory of the Cave, in *The Republic*, is perhaps an even more famous presentation of the distinction between appearances and reality.

Gilbert Ryle's attack on Descartes – with the enjoyable 'Le style c'est Ryle', as J. L. Austin quipped – occurs in his 1949 *The Concept of Mind*. Those days, 'professional' philosophers could proudly write books without giving numerous references and footnotes. Austin – who eclipsed Ryle at Oxford – gave the penguin example in 'Three Ways of Spilling Ink' in his *Philosophical Papers*. The anguished genius lurking behind all this is Ludwig Wittgenstein. His major 'later' work is *Philosophical Investigations* (first published 1953). It was rumoured that Ryle would send his Oxford students to cycle over to Cambridge, where Wittgenstein taught, to learn of the master's latest tormented thinking.

# Chapter Two: Are we responsible for what we do?

A good collection is Gary Watson, ed., *Free Will*, 2nd edn, containing Strawson and Frankfurt. Strawson, although claiming ignorance of determinism, brings forth the importance of reactive attitudes; Frankfurt highlights wantons and levels of desire. For moral luck, the collection suitably entitled *Moral Luck*, ed. Daniel Statman, includes Bernard Williams and Thomas Nagel who set the topic going in recent decades. For existentialism, try Sartre's novel *Nausea* first and his *Existentialism and Humanism*, though later repudiated in part.

# Chapter Three: Surviving

See Raymond Martin and Jonathan Barnes, eds, *Personal Identity*: it contains important papers by Williams and Parfit. Understanding 'the same' as a matter of degree, relating it to personal identity, was argued by Ardon Lyon in 'On Remaining the Same Person', *Philosophy* (1980). See Epilogue below, regarding readings on death.

# Chapter Four: What – morally – ought we to do?

For key readings, old and new, see Fricker and Guttenplan, eds, *Reading Ethics – selected texts with interactive commentary*. Williams' thought-provoking quip 'one thought too many' is in 'Persons, Character and Morality', in his collection *Moral Luck*. If you want originals straightaway, they are Aristotle's *Nicomachean Ethics*, Kant's *Groundwork of the Metaphysics of Morals* and J. S. Mill's *Utilitarianism*.

# Chapter Five: Political philosophy: what justifies the state?

The best introduction is Jonathan Wolff, *An Introduction to Political Philosophy*, 2nd edn. Highly influential classic texts are Thomas Hobbes, *Leviathan*; John Locke, *Second Treatise of Government*; and John Stuart Mill, *On Liberty*. Try Mill first. The recent works used are John Rawls, *A Theory of Justice* (no light read) and Robert

Nozick, *Anarchy, State and Utopia.* Do read G. A. Cohen's slender
2009 work, *Why Not Socialism?* Cohen – 'Jerry' – died in 2009;
he was a great wit and mimic – and transmitted the reply to
Hobbes, given in this chapter. Find him on YouTube.

## Chapter Six: Mind, brain and body

The classic dualism is in Descartes' *Meditations.* For important
papers and surveys of recent work, covering Turing, Searle's
attack, Block *et al,* see J. Heil, ed., *Philosophy of Mind: A Guide and
Anthology* (2003); see also P. M. S. Hacker, *Wittgenstein* (1999).

## Chapter Seven: What, then, is knowledge?

The Wittgenstein quotations are from *Philosophical Investigations*
(1953), §246 and IIxi. The Plato is from his *Meno.* For a wide-
ranging collection of important recent approaches, see Duncan
Pritchard and Ram Neta, eds, *Arguing about Knowledge.* An
approach, seeking to understand knowledge afresh in terms of
information, is Edward Craig's *Knowledge and the State of Nature:
An Essay in Conceptual Synthesis* (1999).

## Chapter Eight: How sceptical should we be?

The Pritchard and Neta knowledge anthology above contains
papers on induction and scepticism. For Popper and research
programmes, a good introduction is Peter Godfrey-Smith's *Theory
and Reality* (2003).

Nelson Goodman introduced 'grue', the new riddle of induction, in his 1954 *Fact, Fiction and Forecast*. For discussion and numerous other paradoxes explained – logical, ethical, epistemic *et al* - see my *This Sentence Is False: an Introduction to Philosophical Paradoxes*. With Saul Kripke, we enter philosophy of language, for which, see Alex Miller's *Philosophy of Language*. An attack on numerous scepticisms is Thomas Nagel's *The Last Word*.

# Chapter Nine: God: for and against

Much written about God is extremely obscure to non-theologians and non-believers. Exceptions – and influential works – are David Hume's *Dialogues Concerning Natural Religion* and John Stuart Mill's *Three Essays on Religion*. An accessible recent sceptical work is Nick Everitt's *The Non-Existence of God*. A good collection of papers, covering religion more generally, is Flint and Rea, eds, *The Oxford Handbook of Philosophical Theology*. A polemical attack against the atheistic line is Edward Fesser's *The Last Superstition* (2010). For an atheist who, thinking a negative cannot be proved, calls himself 'agnostic', try Richard Dawkins, *The God Delusion* where also the Ontological Argument is rejected as mere word play.

# Chapter Ten: The arts: what *is* the point?

For aesthetics, look out for the erudite and thought-provoking Roger Scruton. My comments owe a lot to his *A Very Short Introduction to Beauty*. More generally, see Jerrold Levinson, ed., *The Oxford Handbook of Aesthetics*. The considerable influence of Moore's *Principia Ethica* is described by John Maynard Keynes in his brief *Two Memoirs* (London: Hart-Davis, 1949).

# Epilogue: mortality, immortality and the meaning of life

A wide ranging collection is Cahn and Klemke, eds, *The Meaning of Life*. Bernard Williams' 'The Makropulos case', is in his collection *Problems of the Self*. Thomas Nagel discusses Lucretius, death and life's absurdity in his *Mortal Questions*. My *Humanism: a beginner's guide* (Oneworld) expands points here.

Jean-Paul Sartre speaks of the Other in his *Being and Nothingness*; it is no easy read. Nietzsche's eternal recurrence appears in *The Gay Science*. For Wittgenstein's biography, see the much praised one by Ray Monk, *Ludwig Wittgenstein: the duty of genius* (1990), the excellent one by Brian McGuinness of his early life, *Wittgenstein: 1889–1921* and Rush Rhees, ed., *Ludwig Wittgenstein: Personal Recollections*.

Meaning of life reflections often arise in the arts. A few literary recommendations are Luigi Pirandello's *The Late Mattia Pascal*, Samuel Beckett's plays, for example, *Play* and *Rockaby* and Cavafy's poems. For recent music in addition to *The Death of Klinghoffer* (film version directed by Penny Woolook, 2004), try English National Opera and the operas: John Adams *Nixon in China* and Philip Glass *Satyagraha*. For the more traditional, Schubert's song cycle *Winterreise* (recordings by the recently deceased Dietrich Fischer-Dieskau) is a must as is Britten's *Serenade for Tenor, Horn and Strings* and, yes, Janáček's opera *The Makropulos Case*. Remember, too, that YouTube has online lectures as well as clips of, for example, Bertrand Russell and of the music mentioned.

# Acknowledgements

Having taught philosophy for many years, listened to students' questions and answers – from the bright to the baffling (and they are sometimes identical) – attended papers, also from the baffling to the bright, by philosophers distinguished and undistinguished, it is impossible to give full detailed acknowledgements. Without a doubt, though, I am indebted to numerous students and colleagues, in recent years particularly those associated with The Open University – though in years past also with City University London, University College London and King's College Cambridge.

Philosophers who have wittingly or unwittingly helped over recent years (in no particular order) include Arnold Zuboff, Jerry Valberg, Timothy Chappell, Jonathan Wolff, Derek Matravers, Gerard Livingstone, Michael Clark, Carolyn Price and John Shand. Particular help and/or encouragements have come from philosophers Laurence Goldstein, Raymond Tallis, Sophie Bolat, Martin Holt, Janet Radcliffe Richards - and from Oneworld's Mike Harpley, Ruth Deary and Dawn Sackett. For support over many years, I thank Angela Joy Harvey.

Because of the astonishing amount of noisy building works in Central London the book was mainly written by me, hidden away in The Athenaeum's library; let me thank the ever helpful staff and members and, in particular, Laura Doran for library support, Vanessa Williams for coffee support, and *The Algae*, in particular Dan Cohn-Sherbok and Hazhir Teirmourian, together with Ben Beaumont, for encouraging stimulation on wide-ranging topics.

Special appreciation, as ever, is for Ardon Lyon and his careful reasoning, insightfulness, good humour, competences and even incompetences. Ardon and I both learn a lot from our mistakes and occasionally our thinking aright; sadly, we can both easily forget the latter, not so easily the former – and that thought may remind us again of how our thoughts, our memories – our lives – rest on fortunes, some good, some bad, but both types seemingly ultimately without our control.

Let me add that while writing this book, I was unwittingly developing a cancer, then wittingly undergoing surgical and chemical treatment. I say this not in the search for sympathy (though sympathy is always appreciated), but to encourage an openness about such matters, to promote awareness of improved treatments and, of course, to give immense thanks to the relevant medical and nursing teams at King Edward VII, St Mary's and the Royal Marsden Hospitals in London. Mind you, maybe I ought not to buy long-life milk.

# Index

Bold numbers denote reference to illustrations.

# A Beginner's Guide to Descartes

Harry Bracken expertly summarises Descartes' thoughts on the dualism of mind and body, his "proofs" for God's existence, and his responses to scepticism. Explaining how his life informed his philosophy, Bracken explains the philosopher's enduring significance.

978-1-85168-758-9
£9.99/$14.95

"An engaging, approachable, and informative introduction that will be of great value to anyone approaching Descartes for the first time." **Peter Sedgwick** – Senior Lecutrer in Philosophy, Cardiff University

**HARRY M. BRACKEN** is former Professor of Philosophy at McGill University. In an academic career spanning over 50 years, he has lectured around the world, and is the author of several books and numerous articles on Descartes and related topics.

Browse further titles at
**www.oneworld-publications.com**

# A Beginner's Guide to
# Islamic Philosophy

Tracing the history of the interactions
of philosophy, theology, and mysticism
in Islamic culture, Majid Fakhry's
comprehensive survey follows the
evolution of thought from the
introduction of Greek philosophy
into the Muslim world in the eighth
century right up to the modern era.

978-1-85168-625-4
£9.99

"Provides the reader with an excellent, concise overview of Islamic
philosophy, theology, and mysticism ... Fakhry has accomplished
the task of presenting the central themes and the essence of
1400 years of intellectual tradition in a clear, coherent manner."
*Philosophy East and West*

**MAJID FAKHRY** is Emeritus Professor of Philosophy at the
American University of Beirut, and formerly Lecturer at SOAS,
University of London, Visiting Professor at UCLA, and Associate
Professor of Philosophy, Georgetown University. His publications
include *A History of Islamic Philosophy* (Columbia University
Press), *The Qur'an: A Modern English Version* (Garnet), *Ethical
Theories in Islam* (Brill), *Averroes: His Life, Works and Influence*,
and *Al-Farabi, Founder of Islamic Neoplatonism* (both Oneworld).

Browse further titles at
www.oneworld-publications.com

# A Beginner's Guide to Medieval Philosophy

In this fast-paced, enlightening guide, Sharon M. Kaye takes us on a whistle-stop tour of medieval philosophy, revealing the debt it owes to Aristotle and Plato, and showing how medieval thought is still inspiring philosophers and thinkers today.

978-1-85168-578-3
£9.99/ $14.95

"Beautifully written and wonderfully accessible. Discussing all the major thinkers and topics of the period, Kaye's volume does exactly what it should." **William Irwin** – Professor of Philosophy, King's College Pennsylvania and Editor of *The Blackwell Philosophy and Pop Culture Series*

"Simultaneously entices students into and prepares them for the riches of the abundant literature that lies ready for their exploration." **Martin Tweedale** – Professor Emeritus of Medieval Philosophy, University of Alberta

**SHARON M. KAYE** is Associate Professor of Philosophy at John Carroll University. She is the author of *On Ockham* and *On Augustine*.

Browse further titles at
www.oneworld-publications.com

# A Beginner's Guide to Philosophy of Mind

9781851684786
£9.99/ $14.95

In this lively and entertaining introduction to the philosophy of mind, Edward Feser explores the questions central to the discipline; such as 'do computers think?', and 'what is consciousness?'; and gives an account of all the most important and significant attempts that have been made to answer them.

"A splendid, highly accessible and lucid introduction. The arguments are engaging and provide a refreshing challenge to some of the conventional assumptions in the field."
**Charles Taliaferro** – Professor of Philosophy, St Olaf College, Minnesota

"Fesar has a feel for the enduring problems...an excellent introduction."
**John Haldane** – Professor of Philosophy, University of St Andrews

**EDWARD FESER** is Visiting Assistant Professor of Philosophy at Loyola Marymount University, California, and the author of On Nozick. He has taught and written widely in the areas of philosophy of mind, and his most recent research has focused on new solutions to the mind/body problem

Browse further titles at
www.oneworld-publications.com

Beginners
GUIDES

# A Beginner's Guide to Philosophy of Science

Geoffrey Gorham explores the social and ethical implications of science by linking them to issues facing scientists today: human extinction, extraterrestrial intelligence, space colonization, and more.

9781851686841
£9.99/ $14.95

"Lively, accessible, and clear-headed. Good for the beginning student and for anyone wishing guidance on how to start thinking philosophically about science."
**Helen Longino** – Clarence Irving Lewis Professor of Philosophy, Stanford University

**GEOFFREY GORHAM** has been teaching and researching philosophy of science for 15 years, and is Associate Professor of Philosophy at Macalester College in St. Paul, Minnesota.

Browse further titles at
www.oneworld-publications.com

Beginners GUIDES

# A Beginner's Guide to Philosophy of Religion

Assuming no prior knowledge of philosophy from the reader, Taliaferro provides a clear exploration of the discipline, introducing a wide range of philosophers and covering the topics of morality and religion, evil, the afterlife, prayer, and miracles.

978-1-85168-650-6
£9.99

"Brimming with arguments, the material is cutting edge, and the selection of topics is superb." **J.P. Moreland** – Professor of Philosophy, St Olaf College, Minnesota

"Covers all the most important issues in a way that is always fair-minded, and manages to be accessible without over-simplifying" **John Cottingham** – President of the British Society for the Philosophy of Religion and Professor Emeritus of Philosophy, Reading University

**CHARLES TALIAFERRO** is Professor of Philosophy at St. Olaf College, Minnesota, USA. He is the author or editor of numerous books on the philosophy of religion including as co-editor of *The Blackwell Companion to Philosophy of Religion*.

Browse further titles at
www.oneworld-publications.com